THE SCHMALKALD ARTICLES

THE SCHMALKALD ARTICLES

Martin Luther

Translated by William R. Russell

Fortress Press   **Minneapolis**

THE SCHMALKALD ARTICLES

Cover design: Terry Bentley
Text design: Joseph Bonyata

Library of Congress Cataloging-in-Publication Data

Luther, Martin, 1483–1546.
    [Schmalkaldischen Artikel. English]
    The Schmalkald articles / Martin Luther.
      p. cm.
    Translated by William R. Russell.
    Includes bibliographical references.
    ISBN 0-8006-2661-3 (alk. paper)
    1. Lutheran Church—Creeds—Early works to 1800. 2. Lutheran Church—Doctrines—Early works to 1800. 3. Lutheran Church—Relations—Catholic Church—Early works to 1800. 4. Catholic Church—Relations—Lutheran Church—Early works to 1800. I. Title.
BX8070.S32L8813   1996
238'.41—dc20
                         95-36042
                           CIP

Manufactured in the U.S.A.   AF 1–2661
99   98   97   96   95   1   2   3   4   5   6   7   8   9   10

Contents

Translator's Preface

THE SCHMALKALD ARTICLES IS ONE OF THE MOST SIGNIFICANT DOCUMENTS written by Martin Luther (1483–1545). Its significant stems from the fact that Luther here wrote that he thought was most meaningful and enduring about his theological program. Moreover, because these articles were incorporated into The Book of Concord, they continue to exercise authority in the faith-tradition that bears Luther's name.

Three primary factors give these articles their preeminent position among Luther's prodigious literary output. First, Luther wrote The Schmalkald Articles under the intense pressure of his supposed pending death. His chronic and intense bouts with illness in the mid-1530s caused him and those close to him to fear that he was about to die. In these pages, then, he intended to identify his theological priorities as if this would be his final writing. A sense of existential urgency permeates The Schmalkald Articles and underscores the importance of the theological program they describe. These articles indicate the theological emphases that Luther wanted to bequeath to posterity; they are best seen as his last theological will and testament.

Second, this document reflects Luther's mature theological perspective as he sought to bring order and clarity to his theological program. In the two decades following the posting of the Ninety-Five Theses (1517), Luther was forced to work out his theology in the heat of controversy. Luther spent his public life as an "occasional" theologian who responded to an enormous variety of critics and supporters in greatly differing circumstances. When Luther wrote The Schmalkald Articles, between 1536 and 1538, he had the benefit of some twenty years of public reforming activity behind him.

Third, these articles were intended for use by the sixteenth-century German "evangelicals" as they were preparing to respond to the call of Pope Paul III (1534–1549) to what eventually became the Council of Trent. This gave Luther the opportunity to summarize his own theology and correlate it with his critique of the theology and practice of sixteenth-century Roman Catholicism. In line with the polemical conventions of the day (which may offend some modern sensibilities), Luther evaluated Roman Catholic teaching. In these pages, therefore, we find Luther's views of what needed to be reformed in the church of his time.

The Schmalkald Articles is not a dry theological treatise intended to impress readers with abstract metaphysical musings. It reflects the vitality of Luther's quick mind and personality as they encounter the realities of human life. The reader thereby gains a sense of the person behind the words, a gifted author with a strong response to one of the most tumultuous epochs of human history.

The Articles can and should be used as a key to Luther's central theological concerns. In Part I, "The Lofty Articles of Divine Majesty," the reformer confesses his adherence to the classical creedal Trinitarian tradition of the church catholic. For Luther, the starting point of Christian theology was the threefold revelation of the one God in the Scriptures. This relatively short opening section places all that follows, even Luther's well-known polemical comments on his opponents, in the context of a shared, catholic consensus. This opening section also provides insight into the reformer's self-understanding. Luther did not see himself as an innovator or revolutionary. He simply wanted to call the church of his day back to its own confession. Indeed, he ended Part I with these words: "These articles are not matters of dispute or conflict, for both sides confess them."

In Part II Luther establishes the second pillar of his theology: "The Articles that pertain to the Office and Work of Jesus Christ." Article 1 of Part II is perhaps the most succinct theological definition of Luther's view of the gospel message—at least the reformer himself seemed to think so. He called this statement, "The First and Chief Article," and he concluded by asserting: "We cannot yield or concede anything in this article, even if heaven and earth, or whatever, do not remain." The other three articles of Part II (on the Mass, monastic life, and the papacy) evaluate contemporary teaching and practice by the standard of the gospel confessed in article one.

Part III of the Articles integrates the creedal Trinitarian statement (one might say, the "catholicity") of Part I with the "evangelicalism" of Part II, as Luther applies these priorities to the practice and teaching of the church. The resulting "catholic evangelicalism" stands as a summary of what Luther himself thought was theologically most important about his life's work: the proclamation of the Word as law and gospel and the administration of the sacraments as the means of grace.

The occasion that prompted Luther to write The Schmalkald Articles was the announcement in 1536 by Pope Paul III of a general council of the church to convene in Mantua, Italy in Spring 1537 (as it turned out, this council did not meet at Mantua in 1537, but opened in 1545, at Trent). The primary motivation for the document, however, was the perceived need on the part of Luther and those around him for the reformer to make a definitive theological statement before he died. In a real sense, The Schmalkald Articles is Martin Luther's theological testament.

Abbreviations

AC	The Augsburg Confession.
ACAp	The Apology to the Augsburg Confession.
BC	Theodore Tappert, ed. *The Book of Concord*. Philadelphia: Fortress Press, 1959.
BSLK	*Die Bekenntnisschriften der evangelisch-lutherischen Kirche.* 10th edition. Göttingen: Vandenhoeck & Ruprecht, 1986.
CC	Johann Cochläus. *Ein nötig und christlich bedenck auff des Luther artickeln, die man gemeinem concilio fürtragen sol,* ed. Hans Volz, in *Corpus Catholicorum. Werke Katholischer Schriftsteller im Zeitalter der Glaubensspaltung.* Vol. 18, 1–64. Münster: Verlag der Aschendorffschen Verlagsbuchhandlung, 1932.
CR	*Corpus Reformatorum.* 99 vols. Halle, Berlin, and Leipzig, 1834–.
FCEp	Epitome, Rule and Norm, of the Formula of Concord.
FCSD	Solid Declaration of the Formula of Concord.
LC	The Large Catechism.
LQ	*Lutheran Quarterly,* New Series.
LW	*Luther's Works.* Vols. 1–30, ed. Jaroslav Pelikan. St. Louis: Concordia Publishing House, 1955–86; vols. 31–55, ed. Helmut Lehmann. Philadelphia: Fortress Press, 1955–86.
MSG	Jacques Paul Migne, ed. *Patrologiae Series Graecae.* Paris, 1866–.
MSL	Jacques Paul Minge, ed. *Patrologiae Series Latinae.* Paris, 1844–80.
SA	The Schmalkald Articles.
SC	The Small Catechism.
SCJ	*The Sixteenth Century Journal.*
TCS	The Three Chief Symbols.
Tr	Treatise on the Power and Primacy of the Pope.
UuA	*Urkunden und Aktenstücke zur Geschichte von Martin Luthers Schmalkaldischen Artikeln.* Ed. Hans Volz and Heinrich Ulbrich. Berlin: De Gruyter, 1957.
WA	*D. Martin Luthers Werke. Kritische Gesamtausgabe,* 58 vols. Weimar, 1883–.

WABr	*D. Martin Luthers Werke. Briefwechsel.* 15 vols. Weimar, 1930–.
WADB	*D. Martin Luthers Werke. Deutsche Bibel.* 12 vols. Weimar, 1906–61.
WATR	*D. Martin Luthers Werke. Tischreden.* 6 vols. Weimar, 1912–21.
Walch	Johan G. Walch, ed. *D. Martin Luthers sämmtliche Schriften.* 23 vols. in 25. St. Louis, 1880–1910.
WC	The Wittenberg Concord of 1536. In *The Book of Concord,* vol. 2, 253–56. Philadelphia: General Council Publication Board, 1883.
ZKG	*Zeitschrift für Kirchengeschichte.*
ZST	*Zeitschrift für Systematische Theologie.*
ZTK	*Zeitschrift für Theologie und Kirche, neue Folge.*

The Schmalkald Articles

Martin Luther

Translated and Edited by William R. Russell

ARTICLES OF CHRISTIAN DOCTRINE, WHICH SHOULD HAVE BEEN PRESENTED by our side at the council in Mantua, or wherever else it might happen, and which were to indicate what we could or could not accept or give up, etc. Written by Doctor Martin Luther in the year 1537.[1]

The Preface of Doctor Martin Luther

[1]Pope Paul III called a council to meet at Mantua last year during Pentecost.[2] Afterward he moved it from Mantua, so that we still do not know where he intends to hold it, or whether he can hold it.[3] We on our side had to prepare for the possibility that, whether summoned to the council or not, we would be condemned. I was therefore instructed[4] to compose and collect articles of our teaching in case there was discussion about what and how far we would and could compromise with the papists, and in which things we thought we definitely had to persist and remain firm.

[2]So I collected these articles and presented them to our side.[5] They were

---

1. As a prefatory comment to his own manuscript of SA, Luther wrote this sentence in Latin on the cover: "In these things, there is sufficient doctrine for the life of the church. For the rest, in political and economic matters, there is sufficient law to bind us, so that beyond these burdens there is no need to fashion others. 'Today's trouble is enough for today' [Matt. 6:34]." It was not copied by Spalatin or included in any subsequent versions of SA. The translation here is based on "Die Schmalkaldischen Artikel," ed. Helmar Junghans, in *Martin Luther: Studienausgabe*, ed. Hans-Ulrich Delius (Berlin: Evangelische Verlagsanstalt, 1992), 5:350.

2. Paul III (d. 1549) published the council bull *Ad dominici gregis curam* on June 2, 1536. Pentecost in 1537 fell on May 23.

3. In 1538, when Luther wrote the Preface and published SA, the council had already been postponed twice and did not meet until December 1545 at Trent (Hubert Jedin, *A History of the Council of Trent* [London: Thomas Nelson & Sons, 1957], 1:313–54).

4. John Fredrick gave Luther this assignment on December 11, 1536. (See John Fredrick's letter to the theologians at Wittenberg, *WABr* 7:613f.) The bulk of SA was written during the next two weeks.

5. FCEp 4. It is not clear whether Luther here refers to a December 1536 gathering or select theologians at Wittenberg or to the Bundestag at Schmalkalden in February 1537.

accepted and unanimously confessed by us, and it was resolved that we should publicly present the articles as our confession of faith—if the pope and his adherents should ever become so bold as seriously, genuinely, and without deception or treachery to convene a truly free council,[6] as would be his duty.

[3]But the Roman court is so dreadfully afraid of a free council and so shamefully flees from the light that it has deprived even those who are on the pope's side of their hope that he will ever tolerate a free council, much less actually convene one. They are understandably greatly offended and are troubled when they observe that the pope would as soon see all of Christendom lost and every soul damned as allow himself or his followers to be reformed even a little and permit limits on his tyranny.

Therefore I wanted to make these articles available through the public press at this time, in case I should die before a council could take place (as I fully expect and hope). I wanted to do this, both because the scoundrels, who flee from the light and avoid the day, go to such great pains to postpone and hinder the council, and so that those who live and remain after me will have my testament and confession, in addition to the confession that I have already published.[7] I have held fast to this confession until now and, by God's grace, I will continue to hold to it. [4]What should I say? Why should I complain? I am still alive—every day I write, preach, and teach. Yet there are such poisonous people, not only among the adversaries, but false believers who want to be on our side and who dare to use my writings and doctrine directly against me. They let me look on and listen, even though they know that I teach otherwise. They want to conceal their poison with my work and mislead the poor people by my name. What will happen in the future after my death?[8]

[5]Should I indeed respond to everything while I am still living? Certainly. But then again, how can I alone stop all the mouths of the devil, especially those (they are, however, all poisoned) who do not want to hear or pay attention to what we write? Instead, they devote all their energy to one thing: how they, without any shame at all, might twist and corrupt our words and every letter. I will let the devil (or ultimately God's wrath) answer them as they merit it. [6]I often think of the good Gerson, who doubted whether one should make good writings public. If one does not, then many souls that could have been saved are neglected. But if one does, then the devil is there with innumerable vile, evil mouths that poison and distort everything so that it bears no fruit. [7]Still, what they gain one sees in the daylight. For although they so shame-

---

6. AC, Preface, 21, and *Against the Roman Papacy, an Institution of the Devil,* 1545 (*LW* 41:265–70).

7. *Confession concerning Christ's Supper,* Part III, 1528 (*LW* 37:360).

8. SA, Preface, 3; SA III, 15, 3. *Confession concerning Christ's Supper,* 1528 (*LW* 41:162, 360).

lessly slandered us and wanted to keep the people on their side with their lies, God has continually furthered his work. God has made their number less and less, while our number grows larger and larger. God allows them to be ruined with their lies and continues to do so.

[8]I must tell a story: A doctor, sent here to Wittenberg from France, told us openly that his king was persuaded beyond the shadow of a doubt that there was no church, no government, no marriage among us, but rather everything went on in public as with cattle,[9] and all did what they want. [9]Now imagine, how will we be viewed on that day before the judgment seat of Christ, by those who have represented as pure truth such great lies to the king and to foreign lands through their writings? Christ the Lord and Judge of us all knows quite well that they lie and have lied. They will have to hear the judgment; that I know for sure. May God bring to repentance those who can be converted. For the rest, there will be eternal suffering and woe.

[10]I return to the subject: I would indeed very much like to see a true council, so that many matters and people might be helped. Not that we need it, for through God's grace our churches are now enlightened and supplied with the pure word and right use of the sacrament, an understanding of the various created orders, and true works. Therefore we do not ask for a council for our sakes. In such matters, we know there is nothing good to hope for or expect from the council. Rather, we see in bishoprics everywhere so many parishes empty and deserted[10] that our hearts are ready to break because of it. And yet, neither bishops nor cathedral canons ask how the poor people live or die—people for whom Christ died. And should not these people hear this same Christ speak to them as the true shepherd with his sheep?[11] [11]It horrifies and frightens me that Christ might cause a council of angels to descend upon Germany and totally destroy us all like Sodom and Gomorrah, because we mock him so blasphemously with the council.[12]

[12]In addition to such necessary concerns of the church, there are also innumerable, important things in the secular estate that need improvement: There is disunity among the princes and the estates. Greed and charging interest have burst in like a great flood and have attained a semblance of legality. Recklessness; lewdness; extravagant dress; gluttony; gambling; pompousness;

---

9. This could be a reference to the supposed lewdness of the Wittenbergers.

10. In 1538 it was reported in Wittenberg that there were some six hundred vacant parishes in the bishopric of Würzburg (*WATR* 4:4002). *On the Councils and the Church,* 1539 (*LW* 41:12, 135).

11. John 10:3. SA III, 12, 2.

12. The Latin translation: "pretext of a council." For the story of Sodom and Gomorrah, see Genesis 19.

all kinds of vice and wickedness; disobedience of subjects, servants, workers, all the artisans; extortion by the peasants[13] (who can count them all?) have so taken over that one could not set things right again with ten councils and twenty imperial diets. [13]If participants in the council were to deal with the chief concerns in the spiritual and secular orders that are against God, then their hands would be so full that they would indeed forget the child's games and foolish play of long gowns, large shaved heads,[14] broad cinctures, bishop's and cardinal's hats, crosiers, and similar sleight-of-hand. If we already had fulfilled God's command and precept in the spiritual and secular orders, then we would have found enough time to reform food, clothes, shaved heads, and chasubles. But if we swallow such camels and strain out gnats, let logs stand, and dispute about specks,[15] then we might also be satisfied with such a council.

[14]I, therefore, have provided only a few articles, because we already have received from God so many mandates to carry out in the church, in the government, and in the home that we can never fulfill them. What help is it to make many decretals and regulations in the council, especially if we neither honor nor observe these chief things commanded by God? It is as if we expect God to honor our magic tricks while we trample his real commands underfoot. But our sins burden us and do not permit God to be gracious to us, because we also do not repent and want to defend every abomination.

[15]O dear Lord Jesus Christ, hold a council and redeem your people through your glorious return! The pope and his people are lost. They do not want you. Help us who are poor and miserable, who sigh[16] to you and earnestly seek you, according to the grace you have given us through your Holy Spirit, who with you and the Father lives and reigns, forever praised. Amen.

[PART ONE]

The first part of the articles is about the lofty articles of the divine majesty, namely:

1. That Father, Son, and Holy Spirit, three distinct persons in one divine essence and nature, is one God, who created heaven and earth, etc.

2. That the Father was begotten by no one, the Son was begotten by the Father, the Holy Spirit proceeds from the Father and the Son.

---

13 LC I, 226, 235; *Appeal for Prayer against the Turks,* 1541 (*LW* 43:220); Heerpredigt wider den Türken, 1529 (*WA* 30^{II}:181$_{20ff.}$); *To the Saxon Princes,* 1545 (*LW* 43:279).

14. The distinctive haircut, "the tonsure," worn by medieval monks.

15. Matt. 23:24; 7:3-5.

16. Rom. 8:26.

3. That neither the Father nor the Holy Spirit, but the Son became a human being.

4. That the Son became a human being in this way: he was conceived by the Holy Spirit without male participation and was born of the pure, holy Virgin Mary.[17] After that, he suffered, died, was buried, descended to hell, rose from the dead, ascended to heaven, is seated at the right hand of God, in the future will come to judge the living and the dead, etc., as the Apostles' and the Athanasian symbols,[18] and the common children's catechism, teach.[19]

These articles are not matters of dispute or conflict, for both sides confess them.[20] Therefore it is not necessary to deal with them at greater length.

[PART TWO]

The second part is about the articles that pertain to the office and work of Jesus Christ, or to our redemption.

Here is the first and chief article:[21,22]

[1] That Jesus Christ, our God and Lord, "was handed over to death for our trespasses and was raised for our justification" (Rom. 4[:25]); [2] and he alone is "the Lamb of God, who takes away the sin of the world" (John 1[:29]); and "the Lord has laid upon him the iniquity of us all" (Isa. 53[:6]); furthermore, [3] "All have sinned," and "they are now justified without merit[23] by his grace, through the redemption which is in Christ Jesus . . . by his blood" (Rom. 3[:23-25]).[24]

17. The Latin translation: "always virgin" (*semper virgine*). AC 3, 1 and FCSD 8, 24.

18. Luther uses the Latin word *symbolon*. The creeds were known as "symbols." Cf. TCS I and II. Cf. also *The Three Symbols or Creeds of the Christian Faith*, 1538 (*WA* 50:262–83; *LW* 34:197–229). Regarding Luther's attitude toward the creeds, see F. Kattenbusch, *Luthers Stellung zu den öcumenischen Symbolen* (Giessen, 1883).

19. SC II, 3, 4; LC II, 25–33.

20. In Luther's rough draft of his original manuscript, he had first written, "both parties believe and confess them." Luther's Sermon on Epiphany, January 13, 1538 (*WA* 46:138₁₇f.); *The Three Symbols or Creeds of the Christian Faith*, 1538 (*LW* 34:210f.); *Brief Confession concerning the Holy Sacrament*, 1544 (*LW* 38:310); and Karl Thieme, *Luthers Testament wider Rom in seinen Schmalkaldischen Artikeln* (Leipzig: A. Deichert, 1900), 14–17.

21. AC 2; AC 4: AC 6; AC 20; ACAp 4; SA III, 13; FCEp 3; FCEp 5; FCSD 3; FCSD 5.

22. "Chief article" (German: *Häuptartikel*) is a technical term that Luther uses regularly in SA. His various usages of this word (particularly the use of the prefix *Häupt* or *Haupt* in compounds) indicates a particular item of significance for Luther. *Häupt* is translated here consistently as "chief." Cf. ACAp 4, 2.

23. Luther's translation differs from the Greek, which reads, "as a gift."

24. *WA* 30ᴵᴵ:632f., 636f., 640–43. Here is a so-called satisfaction theory of the atonement (Gustaf Aulen, *Christus Victor* [New York: Macmillan Co., 1969], 81–100).

[4]Now because this must be believed and may not be obtained or grasped otherwise with any work, law, or merit, it is clear and certain that faith alone justifies us.[25] In Romans 3[:26-28], St. Paul says: "For we hold that a person is justified by faith apart from works prescribed by the law"; and also, "that God alone is righteous and justifies[26] the one who has faith in Jesus."

[5]We cannot yield or concede anything in this article,[27] even if heaven and earth, or whatever, do not remain. As St. Peter says in Acts 4[:12]: "There is no other name given among mortals by which we must be saved." "And with his bruises we are healed" (Isa. 53[:5]).

On this article stands all that we teach and practice against the pope, the devil, and the world.[28] Therefore we must be quite certain and not doubt. Otherwise everything is lost, and pope and devil and everything against us will gain victory and dominance.[29]

Article 2

[1]The mass under the papacy has to be the greatest and most terrible horror, as it directly and violently opposes this chief article. Nevertheless it has been the highest and finest of all the various papal idolatries. The papacy contends that this sacrifice or work of the mass (even when done by a rotten rascal) helps people out of sin, both here in this life and beyond in purgatory, even though only the Lamb of God ought and has to do this, as mentioned above, etc. Nothing is to be yielded or given up from this article also, because the first article does not allow it.

[2]And where there were reasonable papists, we would want to speak with them in a friendly way like this: "Why do you hold so firmly to the mass?"

1. Indeed, it is no more than a mere little human invention, not commanded by God. And we are allowed to drop all human inventions, as Christ says in Matthew 15[:9]: "In vain do they worship me with human precepts."

[3]2. It is an unnecessary thing that you can easily omit without sin and danger.

[4]3. You can receive the sacrament in a much better and more blessed way (indeed, it is the only blessed way), when you receive it according to Christ's

---

25. SA III, 13, 1. *On Translating, An Open Letter,* 1530 (*LW* 35:181ff., 187f., 193–99).

26. Luther uses the same word, *gerecht,* to mean both "righteous" and "justifies."

27. The Latin translation: "nor can any believer concede or permit anything contrary to it."

28. *Die Promotionsdisputation von Palladius und Tilemann,* 1537 (*WA* 39[I]:205f.); Explication of Psalm 127:1, 2 (*WA* 40[III]:232).

29. The German word *Recht* is translated here as "dominance."

institution. Why do you want to force the world into misery and destitution for specious reasons, which you have made up (especially when you can have it otherwise in a better and more blessed way)?

[5] Let it be publicly preached to the people that the mass, as a human trifle, may be omitted without sin. No one would be damned who does not observe it but rather would be blessed quite well in a better way without the mass. Indeed, what does it matter if the mass falls of its own accord, not only among the ignorant folk but also among all pious, Christian, reasonable, and God-fearing hearts? How much more would this be the case if they were to hear that the mass is a dangerous thing, fabricated and invented without God's word and will?

[6]4. Because such innumerable, unspeakable abuses have arisen throughout the whole world with the buying and selling of masses, one should rightly give it up (if only to curb such abuses), even if it did have something useful and good in it. Moreover, one should give it up in order to guard forever against such abuses, because it is completely unnecessary, useless, and dangerous—and one can have all things that are more necessary, useful, and certain without the mass.

[7]5. The mass is and can be nothing but a work of a human being (even a rotten rascal), as the canon of the mass and all the books[30] say. One wants to be able to reconcile oneself and others to God, acquire the forgiveness of sins, and merit grace with it (When it is observed in this way, it is observed best. Should it be otherwise?). Thus we should and must condemn and repudiate the mass, because it is directly contrary to the chief article, which says that it is not an evil or devout "Massling" with his work, but rather it is the Lamb of God and Son of God who takes away our sin.[31]

[8]If one would want to "make a good impression,"[32] then one cannot seriously celebrate the sacrament or commune by oneself for the sake of one's personal devotion.[33] If a person seriously desires to commune, then that person administers the sacrament for certain and in the best way according to Christ's institution. However, to commune oneself is a human notion, uncer-

---

30. Liturgical works of the medieval period make reference to "Handing over that which Pope Gelasius, the 50th Primate of Saint Peter, first ordained in the Canon" (Guillaume Durandus, *Rationale divinorum officiorum* [1478], IV:35, 12).

31. John 1:29.

32. The "good impression" here may refer to the communicant's justification before God. Cf. *WA* 50:203 n. 1, and *BSLK* 418 n. 4.

33. Cochläus wrote that private masses are "nowhere forbidden in the Scriptures or by the churches, but rather are much more commanded as can be shown in the Decretals and numerous canons" (*CC*, 16f.).

tain, unnecessary, and even forbidden. Such a person does not know what he or she is doing, because, without God's word, the person is following a false human notion and innovation. [9]Thus it is not correct (even if everything else would otherwise be in order) that one should use the common sacrament of the church for one's own devotional life and play with it to favor oneself without God's word and outside the church community.

[10]This article on the mass will be the sum and substance of the council because, if it were possible for them to concede to us every other article, they could not concede this one. As Campegio said at Augsburg, he would sooner allow himself to be torn to pieces before he would let go of the mass.[34] In the same way I, with God's help, would sooner allow myself to be burned to ashes before I would allow a "Massling" (whether good or evil) and his work to be equal or greater than my Lord and Savior Jesus Christ. Thus we are and remain forever separated and against one another. They rightly recognize this: if the mass falls, the papacy falls. Before they would allow that to happen, they would kill us all, if they could do it.

[11]Moreover, this dragon's tail,[35] the mass, has produced many noxious pests and the excrement of numerous idolatries:

[12]First, purgatory. Because they are occupied with purgatorial masses for the dead and vigils after seven days, thirty days, and a year, and, finally, with the Common Week, All Saints' Day, and Soul Baths, the mass seems only to be used on behalf of the dead, although Christ founded the sacrament only for the living. Purgatory, therefore, with all its splendor, requiems, and transactions, is to be regarded as a manifestation of the devil because it is also against the chief article, that Christ alone (and not human works) ought to help souls. Beyond this, nothing about the dead is commanded or encouraged.[36] For these reasons, one may well want to abandon it, even if it were neither error nor idolatry.

[13]The papists, at this point, use Augustine[37] and some of the fathers, who have supposedly written about purgatory, and think that we do not see why

---

34. Luther mentions this event a number of times: *Dr. Martin Luther's Warning to His Dear German People,* 1531 (*WA* 30^{III}:311$_{25}$; *LW* 47:45); *Glosse auf das vermeinte kaiserliche Edikt,* 1531 (*WA* 30^{III}: 352$_{25-28}$, 362$_{29-31}$); *WATR* 3:3502 (recorded December 12, 1536—precisely while Luther was writing SA) and 3732. Melanchthon had reported on Campegio's strong conviction concerning this point at Augsburg, in 1530 (*CR* 2:168ff., 246ff., 254f.).

35. Rev. 12:3; 20:2. *The Keys,* 1530 (*LW* 40:376).

36. *Confession concerning Christ's Supper,* 1528 (*LW* 37:369).

37. *City of God,* Book 21, chapter 24.

and how they use such passages.[38] Saint Augustine does not write that there is a purgatory and cites no writing that persuades him to it. Instead, he leaves the matter undecided and says simply that his mother asked to be remembered at the altar or at the sacrament.[39] Now all of this is certainly nothing but the human thoughts of a few persons, who can establish no article of faith, which God alone can do. [14]But our papists use such human words in order to make us believe that their shameful, blasphemous, accursed fairs of soul masses make an offering in purgatory, etc. They will never prove such a thing from Augustine. When they have given up their purgatorial "mass fairs" (something Augustine never dreamed of), then we might discuss with them whether Saint Augustine's word, apart from Scripture, ought to be tolerated and whether the dead are to be remembered at the sacrament. [15]It is not valid for them to formulate articles of faith on the basis of the holy fathers' works or words. Otherwise, their food, clothes, houses, etc., would also have to be articles of faith—as they have done with relics. The fact is that[40] God's word should establish articles of faith and no one else, not even an angel.[41]

[16]Second, the result has been that evil spirits have caused much rascality. They have appeared as human souls.[42] They have demanded masses, vigils, pilgrimages, and other offerings with unspeakable lies and cunning, [17]which we all held as articles of faith, according to which we had to live. The pope confirms this, as does the mass along with all the other horrors. Here there is also nothing to yield or surrender.

[18]Third, pilgrimages. Here they also sought masses, the forgiveness of sins, and God's grace. The mass determined everything. Now, it is positively certain that such pilgrimages, without God's word, are not commanded, nor are they necessary. We could have it all in a much better way, without any sin

---

38. Cochläus writes: "We can prove that such a belief and use has been in the Christian church continually from the apostles to the present. Among the Greeks and in the eastern church, St. Dionysius (a disciple of Paul), Origen, Athanasius, Chrysostom, Cyril, Damascus, etc., have borne witness to it. Among the Romans in the western church, the four eminent teachers: Ambrose, Jerome, Augustine, and Gregory bear witness to it along with all other Latin theologians and canons lawyers" (CC, 18–19).

39. *Confessions*, Books 11 and 13.

40. The Latin translation: "We have another rule, namely, that . . ."

41. SA II, 2, 13–15 was not a part of Luther's original manuscript or the copy made by Spalatin and subscribed at Schmalkalden in 1537. Luther inserted this paragraph into the text prior to SA's publication in 1538 (*WA* 50:205–6; *UuA*, 41–42).

42. Luther apparently refers here to the reports of apparitions by Gregory the Great (d. 604), Dialog. IV, chapter 40 (MSL 67, 396f.), and Peter Damian (d. 1072), Opusculum 34, chapter 5 (MSL 145, 578f.).

or danger. We could dispense with it. Why would one allow the neglect of one's own parish, God's word, wives and children, etc., which are necessary and commanded, but run after unnecessary, uncertain, shameful, devilish imps? [19]Only because the devil has taken over the pope, causing him to praise and confirm such practices so that the people are indeed routinely separated from Christ by their own works and become idolaters. Is this not the most evil thing in pilgrimages? Aside from the fact that it is an unnecessary, uncommanded, unwise, and uncertain, and even harmful thing. [20]Here, therefore, there is also nothing to yield or concede, etc. And let it be preached that it is unnecessary as well as dangerous. Then see where pilgrimages stand.[43]

[21]Fourth, fraternities. The monasteries, foundations, and vicars have assigned and conveyed to themselves (by lawful and open sale) all masses, good works, etc., for both the living and the dead. They are not only purely human trifles, without God's word, completely unnecessary and not commanded; but they are also contrary to the first article of redemption, and therefore they can in no way be tolerated.

[22]Fifth, relics.[44] Here a good many open lies and follies are based on the bones of dogs and horses.[45] The devil laughs at such rascality. They should have long ago been condemned, even if there were something good in them. In addition, they are also without God's word, neither commanded nor advised. It is a completely unnecessary and useless thing. [23]The worst is that relics were also to have produced an indulgence and the forgiveness of sin as a good work and act of worship, like the mass, etc.

[24]Sixth, precious indulgences belong here. They are given to both the living and the dead (but for money). The pitiful Judas or pope sells the merits of Christ together with the superabundant merits of all the saints and the entire church, etc. All of this is not to be tolerated, not only because it is without God's word, not necessary, and not commanded; but because it is contrary to the first article. Christ's merit is not acquired through our work or our pennies, but through faith by grace, without any money and merit; not by the authority of the pope, but rather through the sermon or by the preaching of God's word.

On Prayer to Saints

[25]Prayer to the saints is also one of the anti-Christian abuses that is in conflict with the first, chief article and destroys the recognition of Christ. It is

---

43. The Latin translation: "Thus they will spontaneously perish."

44. Cochläus writes that the church fathers, "Jerome . . . , Ambrose, Augustine, Basil, Chrysostom, etc.," approved of relics (*CC*, 25).

45. Luther referred to these supposed bones of the saints in *Predigten des Jahres 1546*, Nr. 4, January 26 (*WA* 51:138$_{5-8}$). Cf. also *On the Councils and the Church*, 1539 (*WA* 50:642$_{23ff}$; *LW* 41:165).

neither commanded nor recommended, has no example from the Scripture, and we have everything a thousand times better in Christ—even if it were a precious possession, which it is not.[46]

[26]Although the angels in heaven pray for us (as Christ himself also does), and in the same way also the saints on earth or perhaps in heaven pray for us, it does not follow from this that we ought to appeal to them; pray; conduct fasts for them; hold festivals; celebrate masses; make sacrifices; establish churches, altars, worship services; and serve them in other ways; and consider them as helpers in need and assign all kinds of aid to them and attribute a specific function to particular saints, as the papists teach and do. That is idolatry. Such honor belongs to God alone. [27]You as a Christian and saint on earth can pray for me, not only in the case of a particular need but in all necessities. But on account of that, I ought not idolize you, appeal to you, hold a celebration, conduct a fast, sacrifice, have a mass in your honor, and base my saving faith on you. I can honor, love, and thank you otherwise quite well in Christ. [28]Now if such idolatrous honor is taken away from the angels and dead saints, then the honor that remains will not hurt anyone, indeed, it will soon be forgotten. When usefulness and help, both physical and spiritual, are no longer expected, then the saints will be left in peace, both in the grave and in heaven. Whether for nothing or out of love, no one will think much about them, esteem them, or honor them.

[29]In summary, we cannot tolerate and must condemn what the mass is, what has resulted because of it, and what depends on it, so that we might hold, use, and receive the holy sacrament by faith, unspoiled and with certainty according to the institution of Christ.

Article 3

[1]In former times, foundations and monasteries were established, with good intentions, for the education of learned people and decent women. They should be returned to such use so that we might have pastors, preachers, and other servants of the church, as well as other necessary persons for earthly government, for the cities and lands, and also well brought up young women to be mothers and housekeepers, etc. [2]Where they are not willing to serve in this way, it is better if one allows them to become deserted or torn down than that they, with their blasphemous worship, established through human beings, should be held as something better than the general Christian vocation and

---

46. Cochläus writes: "We know that praying to saints has been done consistently in the church from the time of the Apostles and it is not forbidden in the Scriptures" (*CC*, 28).

the offices and orders established by God. All this is also contrary to the first and chief article of redemption of Jesus Christ. Furthermore, they (like all other human inventions) are also not commanded, not necessary, not useful— and they make for a dangerous and a vain, futile effort. The prophets call such worship *aven,* which means "empty effort."[47]

Article 4

[1]The pope is not the head of all Christendom "by divine right" or on the basis of God's word[48] (because that belongs only to the one who is called Jesus Christ).[49] The pope is only bishop or pastor of the church at Rome and of those who willingly or through human invention have joined themselves to him (this is his secular authority).[50] They are not under him as a lord, rather beside him as a brother and companion, to be Christians as also the ancient councils[51] and the era of St. Cyprian[52] demonstrate. [2]But now, however, no bishop dares to call the pope "brother," as at that time, but rather must call him his "most gracious lord," as if he were a king or emperor. We will not, ought not, and cannot impose this upon our consciences. But whoever wants to do it, such a person does it without us.

[3]It follows from this that everything which the pope has undertaken and done on the basis of such false, offensive, blasphemous, arrogant power has been and still is a purely diabolical affair and business, which corrupts the

---

47. The Hebrew word *aven* literally means "wickedness," "emptiness," "vanity," "futility." Luther translated it here with *Mühe,* which properly means "effort," "trouble," "labor," "pain." Luther connects *Mühe* with the prophet's denunciation of worship that was "done without feeling and with an evil conscience" (Isa. 1:13, *WADB* 11ˡ:28) and "false teaching and works" (Isa. 29:20, *WADB* 11ˡ:94). *Mühe* is for Luther a technical term (the same word he used in the previous sentence) to point to what he considered to be the vanity (i.e., the *aven*) of monastic life (with its, from Luther's perspective, empty ritual and/or liturgical formality). *Der Prophet Habakuk ausgelegt,* 1526 (*WA* 19:357f.); Isa. 29:20 and 41:29 (*WADB* 11ˡ:94, 127); *Vorlesung über Jesaias,* 1527–30 (*WA* 31ˡˡ:11, 181, 307).

48. Tr 12.

49. Eph. 1:22; 4:15; 5:23; Col. 1:18.

50. This refers to the secular power of the pope, the "patrimony of Peter." 1 Peter 2:13.

51. E.g., the councils of Nicea (A.D. 325), Constantinople (A.D. 381), Ephesus (A.D. 431), and Chalcedon (A.D. 451). Canon IV of the Council of Nicea stipulates that bishops should be elected by their own churches in the presence of one or more neighboring bishops.

52. Cf. Tr. 14. Cyprian (d. 258), as bishop of Carthage, addressed Pope Cornelius as his "very dear brother" (MSL 3:700, 703, 708, 731, 796, 830). Ambrose (d. 397), bishop of Milan, and Augustine (d. 430), bishop of Hippo, addressed the bishops of Rome in their day with similar appellations (MSL 16:1124; MSL 33:758, 764; *Corpus scriptorum ecclesiasticorum latinorum* 44:652, 669).

entire holy Christian church[53] (insofar as it depends on him) and negates the first, chief article on the redemption of Jesus Christ (outside of what belongs to the physical government, through which God allows much good to happen for a people through a tyrant and rascal).

[4] All his bulls and books, in which he roars like a lion (the angel of Revelation 12 indicates this),[54] state that no Christians can be saved unless they are obedient and submit to him in all things—what he wills, what he says, what he does.[55] All of this (which says quite a bit) is nothing other than: "If you believe in Christ and have everything that is necessary for salvation in him, then it is nevertheless nothing and all is vain if you do not hold to me as your god, submit to me and obey." Still, it is obvious that the holy church was without the pope, at the very least, for over five hundred years,[56] and even today the Greek church and many churches that use other languages have never been under the pope and still are not. [5] Thus it is, as it has often been said, a human fiction. It is not commanded. There is no need for it. And it is useless. The holy Christian church can survive quite well without such a head. It would have been much better if such a head had not been raised up by the devil. [6] The papacy is not necessary in the church, because it exercises no Christian office, and the church must continue and exist without the pope.

[7] And I assert that the pope should want to renounce his claim so that he would not be supreme in the church "by divine right" or by God's command. However, in order that the unity of Christendom might be preserved against the sects and heretics, we might accept a head in which all others are held together. Such a head could now be elected by the people and it would remain in their power and by their choice whether to change or depose this head. This is virtually the way the council at Constance handled the popes, deposing the three[57] and electing the fourth. Now I assert (says I) that it is impossible for

---

53. Cf. SA II, 4, 5. "The holy Christian church" is a quotation from the German translations of the Nicene and Apostles' Creeds, which had been used in Germany since the 1400s. Cf. TCS I; TCS II.

54. Luther actually quotes Rev. 10:3. The reformer made the same mistake in *On the Councils and the Church*, 1539 (*WA* 50:578; *LW* 41:90).

55. The most exteme medieval papal claim for such authority is expressed in Boniface VIII's 1302 bull *Unam Sanctam:* "We declare, say, define, and pronounce that it is altogether necessary to salvation for every human creature to be subject to the Roman pontiff" (quoted from *The Book of Concord*, ed. Theodore Tappert [Philadelphia: Fortress Press, 1959], 299 n. 4).

56. Luther thought that Gregory I (d. 604) was the last bishop of Rome prior to the rise of the papacy per se. Tr 19.

57. John XXIII was deposed at Constance on May 29, 1415. Gregory XII abdicated on July 4, 1415. Benedict XIII was deposed on July 26, 1415. Martin V was elected pope on November 11, 1417.

the pope and the chair of Rome to renounce such things and to want to accept this view, because he would have to allow his entire government and order to be overthrown and destroyed with all his laws and books. In summary, he cannot do it.

And even if he were to do it, Christianity would not be helped in any way. There would be many more sects than before, [8]because they would not have to submit to such a head on the basis of God's command but rather from human goodwill. The head of this church would rather easily and quickly be despised, until it would finally have not even one member. It would no longer have to be at Rome or at some other set place,[58] but wherever and in whatever church God would provide a suitable man for it. Oh, that would be a complicated and disorganized setup!

[9]Therefore the church cannot be better ruled and preserved than if we all live under one head, Christ, and all the bishops are equal according to the office—although they may be unequal in their gifts[59]—holding diligently together one unanimous doctrine, creed, sacraments, prayers, and performing works of love, etc. St. Jerome writes that the priests at Alexandria ruled the church together in common, as the apostles also did and afterward all bishops in all of Christendom,[60] until the pope elevated himself over all.

[10]This[61] shows authoritatively that he is the true antichrist or contrachrist, who has raised himself over and set himself against Christ because the pope will not let Christians be saved without his authority, which amounts to nothing. It is not ordered or commanded by God. [11]This is called precisely, "setting oneself over God and against God," as St. Paul says.[62] Neither the Turks nor the Tartars, as great enemies of Christians as they are, do such a thing. They allow whoever desires it to have faith in Christ, and they receive physical tribute and obedience from the Christians.

[12]The pope, however, will not allow faith, but rather says that if one is obedient to him, then one will be saved. We do not intend to do this, even if we have to die in God's name on account of it. [13]All of this stems from his

58. The papal residence had been at Avignon, France, from 1309 to 1377.

59. 1 Cor. 12:4, 8-10; Rom. 12:6-8.

60. Luther refers to two passages from Jerome, which he employs in other contexts as well (e.g., WA 2:228f., 259; WABr 1:392). The citations of Jerome are from *Commentary on the Epistle to Titus*, 1:5, 6 (MSL 26:562); and *Epistle to Euangelus the Presbyter*, no. 146 (MSL 22:1194).

61. The Latin translation of SA: "this doctrine."

62. 2 Thess. 2:4. Luther regularly applied this text to the papacy. Cf. Hans Preuss, *Die Vorstellungen vom Antichrist im späteren Mittelalter, bei Luther und in der konfessionellen Polemik* (Leipzig, 1906), 156.

claim to be head of the Christian church[63] "by divine right." Therefore he has had to set himself up as equal to and even greater than Christ, as the head and lord of the church and, ultimately, the entire world. He allows himself to be called an earthly god and even tries to command the angels in heaven.[64]

[14]And when we distinguish the pope's teaching from that of the Holy Scriptures, or place it next to them, then we find that the pope's teaching, when it is at its best, is taken from the imperial, pagan law[65] and teaches about secular dealings and judgments, as his pronouncements show. Furthermore, they teach about ceremonies involving churches, clothing, foods, persons; along with child's play, fantasies, and foolish activities without number. In all these things, there is absolutely nothing about Christ, faith, and God's commandments.[66]

In the end, this is nothing other than the devil himself who promotes his lies about masses, purgatory, monastic life, one's own works, and worship (which are the essence of the papacy) in contradiction to God. He damns, slays, and plagues all Christians who do not exalt and honor his abominations above all things. Therefore we can no more adore the devil himself as our lord or god than we can allow his apostle, the pope or antichrist, to rule as our head or lord. His papal government is characterized by lying and murder and the eternal ruin of body and soul,[67] as I have demonstrated in many books.[68]

[15]These four articles will furnish them with enough to condemn at the council. They neither can nor will allow us the smallest little portion of these articles. Of this we may be certain. We can depend upon the hope that Christ our Lord has attacked his enemies and will carry the day, both by his Spirit and at his return.[69] Amen.

[16]At the council, we will not stand before the emperor or the secular

---

63. Gratian, *Decretum,* Part I, dist. 21, chap. 3, and dist. 22, chaps. 1–2.

64. On June 27, 1346, Pope Clement VI published the bull *Ad memoriam reducendo,* in which he is said to have commanded the angels "to lead to heaven the souls of the pilgrims who might die on their way to Rome" during the jubilee year of 1350.

65. Luther refers here to Roman law. *WATR* 2:3470.

66. *WATR* 4:4515 and *WATR* 6:6863.

67. FCSD, 10, 20.

68. *Explanations of the 95 Theses,* 1518 (*WA* 1:571; *LW* 31:152); *Proceedings at Augsburg,* 1518 (*WA* 2:20; *LW* 41:281); *The Leipzig Debate,* 1519 (*WA* 2:161; *LW* 31:318); *Disputatio I. Eccii et M. Lutheri Lipsiae habita,* 1519 (*WA* 2:341–43); Letter from Luther to Hieronymus Dungersheim, December 1519 (*WABr* 1:567); Letter from Luther to Hieronymus Dungersheim, December 1519 (*WABr* 1:601–3); Letter from Justus Jonas to Luther, June 1530 (*WABr* 5:432).

69. 2 Thess. 2:8.

authority, as at Augsburg,[70] where they issued a most gracious summons[71] and in goodness allowed the matters to be heard. We will stand before the pope and the devil himself, who does not intend to listen, but only to damn, murder, and drive us to idolatry. Therefore we must not kiss his feet or say, "You are my gracious lord." Rather, we ought to speak as the angel spoke to the devil in Zechariah [3:2], "The Lord rebuke you, O Satan!"

[PART THREE]

We could discuss the following things or articles with learned, reasonable people or among ourselves. The pope and his kingdom do not value these things, because conscience[72] is nothing to them. Money, honor, and power are everything.

[Article 1:] On Sin

[1]First, here we must confess (as St. Paul says in Rom. 5[:12]) that sin is from Adam, the one person through whose disobedience all people became sinners and subject to death and the devil. This is called the original sin, or the chief sin.

[2]The fruits of this sin are the evil works, which are forbidden in the Ten Commandments: unbelief, false belief, idolatry, being without the fear of God, presumption, despair, blindness, and, most of all, not knowing or honoring God. After that, there is swearing with God's name, not praying, not praying for others, not honoring God's word, being disobedient to parents, murdering, promiscuity, stealing, deceit, etc.

[3]This original sin has caused such a deep, evil corruption of nature that reason does not comprehend it; rather, it must be believed on the basis of revelation from the Scriptures[73] (Psalm 50[74] and Rom. 5[:12], Exod. 33[:20], Gen. 3[:6ff.]). The scholastic theologians, therefore, have taught pure error and blindness against this article:

---

70. Luther refers here to the imperial diet that was held at Augsburg in the summer of 1530. It was at that occasion that the Augsburg Confession was presented to Emperor Charles V.

71. On January 21, 1530, Charles V's proclamation for the Diet of Augsburg included these words: "to listen to, understand, and consider each belief, opinion, and viewpoint between us in love and kindness, so that we might come to Christian truth." *Dr. Martin Luther's Warning to His Dear German People*, 1531 (*WA* 30[III]:287, 292; *LW* 47:24f., 30).

72. Luther uses a Latin word, *conscientia*.

73. FCEp 1, 9.

74. The Vulgate (Latin Bible) numbered the Psalms differently from modern English versions. Here Luther refers to Ps. 51:6-7.

[4]First, that after the fall of Adam, the natural powers of human beings were still whole and uncorrupted. As the philosophers[75] taught, a person had, by nature, sound reason and goodwill.

[5]Second, that the human being has a free will, either to do good and reject evil or to reject good and do evil.[76]

[6]Third, that the human being could, by using natural powers, keep and carry out every command of God.

[7]Fourth, that human beings could, from natural powers, love God above all things[77] and their neighbors as themselves.

[8]Fifth, that if a person does as much as possible, then God will certainly give grace to that person.[78]

[9]Sixth, that if someone wants to go to the sacrament, it is not necessary to have a proper intention to do good, but it is enough for that person not to have an evil intention to commit sin,[79] because nature is so completely good and the sacrament is so powerful.

[10]Seventh, that there is no basis in Scripture that the Holy Spirit with his grace is necessary for a good deed.[80]

[11]These and many similar things have come from a lack of understanding and ignorance about both sin and Christ our Savior. We cannot allow these purely pagan teachings, because, if these teachings were right, then Christ died in vain.[81] There would be no guilt or sin in humankind for which he had to die—or he would have died only for the body and not for the soul, because the soul would be healthy and only the body would be mortal.

[Article 2:] On Law

[1]We maintain here that the law has been given by God, in the first place, to curb sin by means of the threat and terror of punishment and also by means of the promise and offer of grace and favor. All of this failed because of the evil which sin worked in humankind. [2]Some became worse because of it. They are, therefore, enemies of the law, which prohibits what they want to do

---

75. E.g., Plato (d. 347 B.C.) and Aristotle (d. 322 B.C.).

76. FCSD 2, 33.

77. E.g., John Duns Scotus (d. 1308), *Commentary on the Sentences,* III, Distinction 27, Question 1.

78. E.g., Gabriel Biel, sent. II, d 27 q i, art. 3, dub. 3 0. Cf. also Heiko Oberman, *The Harvest of Medieval Theology* (Durham, N.C.: Labyrinth Press, 1983), 468.

79. Cf. SA III, 3, 17, and the note in that place.

80. FCSD 2, 33.

81. Gal. 2:21.

and commands what they do not want to do. On account of this, where they are not restrained by punishment, they do more against the law than before. These are the coarse, evil people who do evil whenever they have an opportunity.

[3]Others become blind and presumptuous, allowing themselves to think that they can and do keep the law by their own powers (as has just been said above about the scholastic theologians).[82] This attitude results in hypocrites and false saints.

[4]The foremost office or power of the law is that it reveals original sin and its fruits.[83] It shows human beings how deeply they have fallen and how their nature is completely corrupt. The law must say to them that they have no God. They honor or worship strange gods. This is something that they would not have believed before without the law. Thus they are terrified, humbled, despondent, and despairing. They anxiously desire help but do not know where to find it. They become enemies of God, murmuring,[84] etc. [5]This is what is meant by Romans [4:15]: "The law brings wrath,"[85] and Romans 5[:20] "Sin becomes greater through the law."

[Article 3:] On Repentance

[1]The New Testament maintains this office of the law and teaches it, as Paul does and says, in Romans 1[:18]: "The wrath of God is revealed from heaven against all."[86] Also Romans 3[:19-20]: "So that the whole world is guilty before God" and "no human being will be justified in his sight"; and Christ says in John 16[:8]: The Holy Spirit "will convince the world of sin."

[2]Now this is the thunderclap of God, by means of which both the obvious sinner and the false saint[87] are destroyed.[88] God allows no one righteousness and drives them altogether into terror and despair. This is the hammer (as Jer. [23:29] says): "My word is a hammer which breaks the rocks to pieces."

---

82. SA III, 1, 6.

83. Rom. 3:20; 7:7; SA III, 1, 3.

84. Rom. 5:10; Exod. 16:8; Luke 15:2; 19:7.

85. Luther mistakenly refers to Romans 3.

86. Cf. FCSD 5, 14.

87. Cf. SA III, 2, 2–3.

88. This metaphor is an echo of Luther's famous 1508 encounter with the lightning bolt on the outskirts of Stotternheim. This event prompted him to enter the monastery. Cf. Roland H. Bainton, *Here I Stand: A Life of Martin Luther* (New York: New American Library, 1950), 15. SA III, 3, 30.

This is not "active contrition,"[89] a contrived remorse, but "passive contrition,"[90] the true suffering of the heart, the suffering and pain of death.

[3]This is what is known as the beginning of true repentance. Here a person must listen to a judgment such as this: "There is nothing in any of you—whether you appear publicly to be sinners or saints.[91] You must all become something other than what you are now, and act in another way, no matter who you are now and what you do. You may be as great, wise, powerful, and holy as you could wish, but here no one is godly," etc.[92]

[4]To this office of the law, however, the New Testament immediately adds the consoling promise of grace through the gospel.[93] This we should believe. As Christ says in Mark 1[:15]: "Repent and believe in the good news."[94] This is the same as, "Become and act otherwise, and believe my promise." [5]And before Jesus, John the Baptizer was called a preacher of repentance—though for the forgiveness of sins. That is, he convicted them all and made them into sinners, so that they would know what they were before God and would recognize themselves as lost people. In this way they were prepared for the Lord. They received the forgiveness of sins expectantly and receptively. [6]Jesus himself says in Luke [24:47]: "You must preach repentance and forgiveness of sins in my name to all nations."

[7]But where the law exercises such an office alone, without the assistance of the gospel, there is[95] death and hell. Humankind has to despair, like Saul and Judas, as St. Paul says: "The law kills through sin."[96] [8]On the other hand, the gospel does not give consolation and forgiveness in only one way—but rather through the word, sacraments, and the like (as we shall hear). With God, there is truly rich redemption from the great prison of sin (as Psalm 129 [130:7-8] says).

[9]Now we must compare the false penance of the sophists with true repentance, in order that they both might be better understood.[97]

---

89. Luther uses a Latin phrase, *activa contritio.*

90. Luther uses a Latin phrase, *passiva contritio.*

91. The Latin translation: "in your own opinion."

92. Rom. 3:10-12. See also SA III, 3, 33.

93. FCSD 5, 14. *WA* 7:24.

94. See also Matt. 3:2; Luke 3:15.

95. The Latin translation: "nothing else but."

96. Rom. 7:10; for Saul, see 1 Sam. 28:20 and 31:4; for Judas, see Matt. 27:3-5.

97. Cochläus writes, "[Luther] leaves out the beginning, middle, and end of the true gospel that, above all, teaches us to do Penance" (*CC,* 42).

On the False Penance of the Papists[98]

[10]It is impossible that they should teach correctly about penance, because they do not recognize true sin. As mentioned above,[99] they hold nothing right about original sin, but rather they say that the natural powers of humankind have remained whole and uncorrupted. They say that reason can teach correctly and the will can rightly act according to it. They say that God surely gives his grace if a person does as much as is within that person, according to human free will.

[11]From this it must follow that they only do penance for actual sins, such as evil thoughts to which they consent (because evil impulses, lust, and inclinations were not sin), evil words, and evil works (which they could have well avoided by means of their free will).

[12]They divide such penance into three parts.[100] There is remorse, confession, and satisfaction, with the following comfort and pledge: if a person experiences true remorse, confesses, and makes satisfaction, then that person, by these actions, merits forgiveness and pays for sins before God. In this way, they have instructed the people who come to penance to have confidence in their own works. [13]From this came the phrase that was spoken from the pulpit when they said the general confession on behalf of the people: "Spare my life, Lord God, until I might repent of my sins and improve my life."[101]

[14]Here there was no Christ. Nothing was mentioned about faith, but they hoped to overcome and wipe out sin before God with their own works. We also become priests and monks with this intention: we wanted to set ourselves against sin.

[15]Remorse was handled in this way: because no one could recall all of one's sins (particularly those of an entire year),[102] the person found another way out.[103] If an unknown sin was remembered later, then one was also to be remorseful for it and confess it, etc. Meanwhile, one was commended to God's grace.

[16]Moreover, since no one knew how great the remorse should be, so

---

98. ACAp 12, 98–178.

99. SA III, 1, 4–11.

100. Luther discusses these three respective parts of repentance in what follows: SA III, 3, 12–21.

101. This phrase, or its equivalent, dates back to at least the tenth century and was spoken by the pastor, in behalf of the congregation, at the conclusion of the sermon. *BSLK* 439 n. 3.

102. At the Fourth Lateran Council (1215), it was stipulated that all who had reached the age of discretion (seven years) must confess their sins to a priest at least once a year.

103. Luther uses an idiom, which, translated literally, is, "they mended the coat" or "patched the hide" (*flickten sie den Pelz*).

that one might certainly have enough before God, one was given this comfort: whoever could not have contrition,[104] that is, have remorse, then that person should have attrition.[105] I like to call this a halfway or beginning remorse because they themselves have not as yet understood either word and they still know even less about what they mean than I do. Such attrition was counted as contrition when they went to confession.

[17]And when it happened that some said they could not repent or be sorrowful for their sins, as might happen in fornication or revenge, etc., they were asked whether they at least wished or willingly desired to have remorse. When they would say "yes" (because who would say "no," except the devil himself?), it was considered to be remorse and their sins would be forgiven on the basis of such a good work. Here they pointed to St. Bernard as an example, etc.[106]

[18]Here we see how blind reason stumbles into the things of God and seeks comfort in its own works, according to its own presumption. It cannot think about Christ or faith. If we look at this now in the light, then such remorse is a contrived and imaginary idea. It comes from one's own powers, without faith, without knowledge of Christ. Given this, a poor sinner who had thoughts of lust or revenge would have rather laughed than cried, except if the person had truly confronted the law or been plagued by the devil with a sorrowful spirit. Otherwise, it is certain that such remorse would be pure hypocrisy and would not kill the desire for sin. The person had to have remorse, but would rather sin more—if it would have been without consequences.

[19]Confession was like this: everyone had to enumerate all of one's sins (which is an impossible thing). This was a great torment. Whatever the person had forgotten could be forgiven only when it was remembered—and then it still had to be confessed. With that, one could never know whether one had confessed perfectly enough or whether confession could ever end. At the same time, people were pointed to their works and told that the more perfectly they confessed and the more ashamed they were and the more they humbled themselves before the priest, the sooner and better they would do enough to deal with their sin. Such humility would certainly earn the grace of God.[107]

[20]Here also there was neither faith nor Christ, and the power of the

---

104. Luther uses a Latin word: *contritionem.*

105. Luther uses the Latin word: "attrition." Regarding the scholastic theory of *contritio* and *attritio,* see O. Scheel, *Martin Luther* (1930), 288f.

106. *Treatise on Grace and Free Will,* IV, 10 (MSL 182, 1007).

107. Cf. Peter Abelard (d. 1142), *Ethica seu scito te ipsum,* chap. 24 (MSL 178, 668), and *Epitome theologiae christianae,* chap. 36 (MSL 178, 1756).

absolution was not told to them. Rather, their comfort was based on the enumeration of sins and humiliation. It is not possible to count what torments, rascality, and idolatry such confession produced.[108]

[21]Satisfaction is truly the most intricate[109] of the three because no one could know how much should be done for each individual sin, much less for all sins. Here they came up with only one bit of advice: impose a few satisfactions, which one could easily uphold, such as saying the Lord's Prayer five times, fasting for a day, etc. They then directed those with leftover penance to purgatory.

[22]Here, as well, there was only pure misery and destitution. Some imagined that they would never get out of purgatory because, according to the ancient canons, each mortal sin carried with it seven years of penance.[110] [23]Still, confidence was placed on our work of satisfaction and, if the satisfaction would have been perfect, then confidence would have been placed totally upon it and neither faith nor Christ would be of any use. But this confidence was impossible. If they would have done penance for a hundred years in this way, they would still not have known whether they were penitent enough. This means always doing penance but never arriving at repentance.

[24]At this point, the holy chair of Rome[111] established indulgences in order to help the poor church.[112] With these, the pope forgave and remitted the satisfaction, first for seven years in a particular case, and then for a hundred years, etc. The indulgences were then divided among the cardinals and bishops, so that one could grant a hundred years and another could grant a hundred days. However, the pope reserved for himself the right to remit the entire satisfaction.[113]

[25]Only after this practice began to bring in money and the market in bulls became lucrative did the pope come up with the jubilee year and attach it to Rome—which offered the forgiveness of all penalties and guilt.[114] The people came running, because everyone wanted to be set free from the

---

108. The Latin translation inserts a reference to Chrysostom's "Sermon on Penance" (MSG 48, 754).

109. The Latin translation: "perplexing."

110. *47 canones poenitentiales,* by Astesanus (d. 1330).

111. The pope, as head of the church, was seen as the occupant of the chair or throne (Latin: *cathedra*) of St. Peter.

112. "The poor church" appears to be a reference to the sad state to which churchly penance had deteriorated as well as an ironic reference to the financial situation in Rome.

113. Plenary indulgences were instituted in 1095 by Pope Urban II in connection with the first crusade.

114. Luther refers here in German to the Latin expression *remissio poenae et culpae,* which dates back liturgically to the mid-thirteenth century.

heavy, unbearable burden. This is called "finding and digging up the treasures of the earth."[115] Immediately, the popes pressed further and established many jubilee years to follow one another. The more money he swallowed, the wider the pope's gullet became. Therefore he sent his legates across the lands, until all the churches and every home were influenced by the jubilee year. [26]Finally, he squeezed into purgatory with the dead—first with masses and the establishment of vigils; after that, with indulgences and the jubilee year. In the end, souls became so cheap that one could be sprung for a nickel.[116]

[27]That still did not help anything. Although the pope taught the people to rely on and trust in such indulgences, he himself once again made the process uncertain when he asserted in his bulls, "Whoever desires to partake of the indulgence or the jubilee year should be remorseful, go to confession, and give money."[117] We have heard above that such remorse and confession were uncertain and hypocritical.[118] Similarly, no one knew which soul might be in purgatory and no one knew which few had felt real remorse and confessed. In this way, the pope took the money and comforted them with his authority and indulgence and still directed them to their uncertain works.

[28]Now, there were a few who did not consider themselves guilty of any real sins (that is, of thoughts, words, and deeds), myself and others like me, who wanted to be monks and priests in monasteries and foundations. We fasted, kept vigils, prayed, held masses, used rough clothing and furniture, etc., in order to resist evil thoughts. With earnestness and intensity we wanted to be holy. Still, the hereditary, inborn evil did something while we slept, which is its manner (as St. Augustine[119] and St. Jerome,[120] along with others, confess). Each one still held that some of the others were so holy, as we taught, that they were without sin and full of good works. On this basis, we transferred and sold our good works to others, since we did not need them all to get to heaven. This is certainly true, and there are seals, letters, and examples available.

[29]Such people do not need repentance, because, if they do not consent

115. Dan. 11:43. Christians in the medieval and late medieval period used this passage to express their conviction that the devil would show the antichrist where the concealed riches of the earth were hidden, so that the people could bring them to the antichrist (Preuss, *Die Vorstellungen vom Antichrist im späterem Mittelalter,* 20).

116. Luther apparently refers to the infamous verse of the indulgence preachers: "When the coin in the coffer rings, the soul from purgatory springs!"

117. Penance and confession, beginning in the middle of the thirteenth century, were regularly connected with indulgences.

118. SA III, 3, 16–23.

119. *Confessions,* Book II, Chapter 2, and Book X, Chapter 30.

120. *Epistle to Eustochius* 22:7.

to evil thoughts, then for what would they be remorseful? What would they confess, when they avoid evil words? For what would they want to make satisfaction, when their deeds were guiltless? They could sell their over-and-above righteousness to other, poor sinners. The Pharisees and scribes in the time of Christ were such saints.[121]

[30]At this point, the fiery angel St. John, the preacher of true repentance, comes to destroy everyone together with a single thunderclap, saying, "Repent!"[122] Some people think this way: "We have already done penance." [31]Others think: "We do not need repentance." [32]John says, "All of you together repent! On the one hand, you are false penitents; on the other hand, they are false saints. You all need the forgiveness of sins because you all still do not know what true sin is, let alone that you ought to repent of it or avoid it. You are no good. You are full of unbelief, stupidity, and ignorance regarding God and his will. Because God is present here, we all must receive grace upon grace from his fullness,[123] and no human being can be justified before God without it. Therefore, if you want to repent, then repent in the right way. Your penance does not do it. You are hypocrites who think you do not need repentance.[124] You are a brood of vipers.[125] Who assured you that you will escape the wrath to come?" etc.[126]

[33]St. Paul also preaches this way in Romans 3[:10-12] and says, "No one has understanding." "No one is righteous." "No one seeks God." "No one does good, not even one. They have become worthless and forsaken." [34]Also, Acts 17[:30]: "But now God commands all people everywhere to repent." He says, "all people"—no single human being is excluded. [35]This repentance teaches us to recognize sin; that is, we are all lost. Neither hide nor hair of us is good and we must become absolutely new people.

[36]This repentance is neither incomplete and partial, like that which does penance for actual sins, nor is it uncertain. It does not deliberate over what is a sin or what is not a sin. Instead, it simply lumps everything together[127] and

---

121. The Latin translation: "and hypocrites."

122. Matt. 3:2. Regarding the fiery angel, see Mal. 3:1 and M. Henschel, "'Der feurige Engel S. Johannes': Zu einer Stelle in Luthers Schmalkaldischen Artikeln," *Lutherjahrbuch* 31 (1964): 76. See also Matt. 11:10 and SA III, 3, 2.

123. John 1:16.

124. In the last two sentences, Luther makes a wordplay with *Busse*, using it to mean both "penance" and "repentance."

125. Matt. 3:7.

126. Matt. 3:7; Luke 3:7.

127. Luther uses an idiom, "*stosst alles in Haufen.*"

says, "Everything is pure sin with us." What is it that we would want to spend so much time searching, dissecting, or distinguishing? Therefore, here as well, remorse is not uncertain, because there remains nothing that we would like to consider as a possession that could pay for sin. Rather, there is plain, certain despair about all that we are, think, say, or do, etc.

[37]Similarly, such confession also cannot be false, uncertain, or partial. Whoever confesses that "everything is pure sin with them"[128] bring together all sins and allow no exceptions. None are forgotten. [38]Thus satisfaction is also not uncertain. It is not our uncertain, sinful work but rather the suffering and blood of the innocent "Lamb of God, who takes away the sin of the world."[129]

[39]John preached about this repentance and, after him, Christ in the Gospels, and we also. With this repentance, we knock to the ground the pope and everything that is built upon our good works, because it is all built upon a rotten, flimsy basis: good works or law. There are no good works, only purely evil works. No one keeps the law (as Christ says in John 7[:19]), but all transgress it. Therefore the structure is merely false lies and hypocrisy, even when it is most holy and at its best.

[40]This repentance endures among Christians until death because it confesses the sin that remains in the flesh throughout life.[130] As St. Paul bears witness in Romans 7[:23], he wars with the law in his members, etc., and he does this not by using his own powers but with the gift of the Holy Spirit which follows the forgiveness of sins.[131] This same gift daily cleanses and expels the sins that remain and works to make people truly pure and holy.[132]

[41]The pope, theologians, lawyers, and all human beings know nothing about this. Rather, it is a doctrine from heaven, revealed through the gospel, and the godless saints are forced to call it heresy.

[42]Some fanatical spirits might come again. (Perhaps some already are at hand, just as I saw for myself at the time of the disturbance.)[133] They maintained that, if any who once receive the Spirit or the forgiveness of sin or become a believer, might sin after that, then such sin would not hurt those who

128. SA III, 3, 36.
129. John 1:29. See also SA II, 1, 2.
130. FCSD 2, 34–35.
131. Rom. 8:2.
132. Cf. SC IV, 12; FCSD 2, 33–34.

133. Luther's view of the "spirits" and "enthusiasts" was colored by the disturbances at Wittenberg in the early 1520s, led by Andreas von Karlstadt and "the Zwickau prophets," Thomas Münzer and the Peasants' War [1525], and "The Kingdom of God" at Münster [1534–35].

continue to remain in faith. They shout, "Do what you will! If you believe, then nothing matters. Faith eradicates all sin," etc. They say, in addition, that if someone sins after receiving faith and the Spirit, then that person never really had the Spirit and faith. I have seen many such people and I am concerned that such a devil is still in some.

[43]Therefore it is necessary to know and teach that when holy people somehow fall into a public sin (such as David, who fell into adultery, murder, and blasphemy against God), then faith and the Spirit have left (this sets aside the fact that they still have and feel original sin and also daily repent of it and struggle against it). The Holy Spirit does not allow sin to rule and dominate so that a person acts on it, but the Spirit controls and resists, so that sin is not able to do what it wants. However, if sin does what it wants, then the Holy Spirit and faith are not there. As John says (1 John 3:9; 5:18): "Those who have been born of God do not sin and cannot sin." And it is still the truth (as the same St. John writes [1:8]): "If we say we have no sin, we deceive ourselves, and the truth of God is not in us."[134]

[Article 4:] On the Gospel[135]

We now want to return to the gospel, which gives more than just one kind of counsel and help against sin, because God is overwhelmingly rich in his grace: first, through the spoken word, in which the forgiveness of sins is preached to the whole world (which is the particular office of the gospel); second, through Baptism; third, through the Holy Sacrament of the Altar; fourth, through the power of the keys and also the mutual conversation and consolation of the brothers and sisters.[136] Matthew 18[:20]: "Where two or three are gathered," etc.[137]

---

134. SA III, 3, 42–45 was added to the text by Luther as he prepared the document for publication in 1538. The emphasis here would seem to be directed against John Agricola and the "antinomians," who taught that the law did not apply to Christians. There was a heated controversy over this issue among the Wittenberg theologians in the middle and late 1530s. These paragraphs were not part of the document Agricola subscribed in December of 1536. Cf. Die Schmalkaldischen Artikel, 1537, 1538 (WA 50:239f.); Zangemeister, Die Schmalkaldischen Artikel, 65f.

135. From this point forward, because of an apparent heart attack, Luther was forced to dictate the rest of SA. Caspar Cruciger recorded SA III, 4–9 and 13–15. Another, unknown secretary recorded SA III, 10–12. R. Wetzel, "Casper Cruciger als ein Schreiber der 'Schmalkaldischen Artikel,'" Lutherjahrbuch 54 (1987), 92.

136. Luther uses a Latin phrase: per mutuum colloquium et consolationem fratrum. The origin of this formula is obscure.

137. Luther wrote: "Where two are gathered."

[Article 5:] On Baptism

[1]Baptism is nothing other than the word of God in water, commanded by God's institution, or, as Paul says, "washing in the word." [138] Moreover, Augustine says, "When the word has been added to the element it makes a sacrament." [139] [2]Therefore we do not agree with Thomas[140] and the Dominicans who forget the word (God's institution) and say that God has placed a spiritual power in the water which, through the water, washes away sin. [3]We also do not agree with Scotus[141] and the Franciscans who teach that baptism washes away sin through the assistance of the divine will, that this washing takes place only through God's will, and this is not at all through the word and the water.

On the Baptism of Children

[4]We maintain that we should baptize children because they also belong to the promised redemption which was accomplished through Christ.[142] The church ought to extend it to them.

[Article 6:] On the Sacrament of the Altar

[1]We maintain that the bread and the wine in the supper are the true body and blood of Christ[143] and they are extended to and received not only by pious but also by evil Christians.[144]

[2]And one should not give only one form of the sacrament. And we do not need the lofty science that was taught to us, that as much is given in one form as is given in both. This is how the sophists and the Council of Constance teach.[145] [3]Even if it were true that as much is given with one as with both,

---

138. Luther quotes a Latin version of Eph. 5:26: *lavacrum in verbo.*

139. *Tractate 80,* on John 3 (MSL 35, 1840). Augustine's actual words were, "When the word is added to the element it makes a sacrament." Luther referred to this statement in other contexts: LC IV, 18; LC V, 10. Cf. also *Luther, Aufzeichnung über Augustins Worte: "Accedat verbum ad elementum et fit sacramentum,"* no date (*WABr* 12:399–401).

140. Thomas Aquinas, *Summa theologiae,* III, Question 62, Article 4.

141. John Duns Scotus (d. 1308), *Commentary on the Sentences* IV, Distinction 1, Question 2.

142. Matt. 19:14.

143. In Luther's rough draft of his original manuscript, he had first written, "We maintain that under the bread and the wine in the supper there is the body and blood of Christ." WC reads, "with the bread and wine the body and blood of Christ are truly and substantially present, offered and received. . . . The bread is the body of Christ." AC 10, 1; *WA* 50, 242.

144. WC reads, "the unworthy also eat, so they hold that the body and blood of the Lord are truly extended also to the unworthy, and that the unworthy receive, where the words and institution of Christ are retained." *BSLK,* 451 n. 1.

145. *WA* 39^i:13–38.

one kind is still not the complete order and institution as founded and commanded by Christ. [4]Especially do we condemn and curse, in God's name, those who not only allow distribution in both forms to be omitted but also haughtily prohibit, condemn, and slander both forms as heresy. Thus they set themselves against and above Christ, our Lord and God, etc.

[5]We have absolutely no regard for the subtle sophistry[146] concerning transubstantiation. They teach that bread and wine leave or lose their natural substances and only the form and color of the bread remain, but is no longer real bread. It is closest to Scripture to say that bread is and remains there, as St. Paul himself indicates: "The bread that we break" and "Eat of the bread."[147]

[Article 7:] On the Keys

[1]The keys are an office and authority given to the church by Christ[148] to bind and loose sins. These are not only the rude and well-known sins but also the subtle, secret ones that only God knows. As it is written, "But who can detect one's own errors?"[149] And Paul himself complains in Romans 7[:23] that he served, with his flesh, the "law of sin." [2]It is not within our power, but it is God's alone, to judge which, how great, and how many sins there are. As it is written: "Do not enter into judgment with your servant, for no one living is righteous before you."[150] And Paul also says in 1 Corinthians 4[:4]: "I am not aware of anything against myself, but I am not thereby acquitted."

[Article 8:] On Confession

[1]Because absolution or the power of the keys is a comfort and help against sin and a bad conscience, and was instituted by Christ in the Gospel,[151] confession and absolution should by no means be allowed to fall into disuse in the church—especially for the sake of weak consciences and young, immature people who are being examined and instructed in Christian doctrine.

[2]The enumeration of sins, however, ought to be free for each individual with respect to what each one wants or does not want to enumerate. As long as we are in the flesh we will not lie if we say, "I am a poor person, full of sin."[152] Romans 7[:23] puts it this way: "I feel in my members another law."

---

146. In 1520, Luther called transubstantiation an "illusion of St. Thomas and the pope" (*The Babylonian Captivity of the Church, WA* 6:456$_{36}$; *LW* 44:199).

147. 1 Cor. 10:16; 11:28.

148. Matt. 16:19; 18:18.

149. Ps. 19:12.

150. Ps. 143:2.

151. Matt. 16:19.

152. 2 Esdras 7:68.

Because private absolution[153] is derived from the office of the keys, we should not neglect it but hold it in high esteem and worth, just as all the other offices of the Christian church.

[3]In these things, which concern the spoken, external word, it is certain to maintain this: God gives no one his Spirit or grace apart from the external word which goes before. We are thus protected from the enthusiasts, that is, the spirits, who boast that they have the Spirit apart from and before contact with the word. They judge the Scriptures or the word accordingly, interpreting and stretching them however it pleases them. Münzer did this, and there are still many who do this today. They want to be shrewd judges between the spirit and the letter, but they do not know what they say or teach.[154] [4]The papacy is also pure enthusiasm. The pope boasts that "all laws are in the shrine of his heart"[155] and that what he decides and judges in his churches is supposed to be spirit and law—as if it is equal to or above the Scriptures or the spoken word.[156] [5]All of this is the old devil and old snake which also made Adam and Eve into enthusiasts. The devil led them from the external word of God to "spirituality" and their own presumption—and even this was still accomplished by means of other, external words. [6]Similarly, our enthusiasts also condemn the external word, but they themselves still do not keep silent. They chatter and write so as to fill the world—as if the Spirit could not come through the Scriptures or the spoken word of the apostles. But the Spirit must come through their writings and words. Why do they not abstain from their preaching and writing until the Spirit himself comes into the people apart from and in advance of their writings? They boast that the Spirit has come into them without the preaching of the Scriptures. There is no time here to debate these matters more extensively. We have dealt with them sufficiently elsewhere.

[7]Also, both those who believe prior to baptism and those who receive faith in baptism have it through the external word which goes before. Adults who have reached the age of reason must have already heard, "Whoever believes and is baptized will be saved,"[157] even though they were at first without faith and after ten years received the Spirit and baptism. [8]In Acts 10[:1ff.], Cornelius had for a long time heard from the Jews about a future Messiah, through whom he would be justified before God. His prayers and alms were

153. Luther uses a Latin phrase: *absolutio privata*.
154. AC 5, 4.
155. *Corpus juris canonici*, Book VI, I, 2, c. 1.
156. Tr 6.
157. Mark 16:16.

acceptable in such faith (Luke calls him "righteous and God-fearing [10:2, 22]), and not without such a preceding word or hearing could there be faith or righteousness. But St. Peter had to reveal to him that the Messiah (on whose future coming he had, until then, believed) now had come. His faith in the future Messiah ought not hold him captive along with the hardened,[158] unbelieving Jews, but he ought to know that he now needs to be saved by the present Messiah and not, like the Jews, deny or persecute him.

[9]In summary: enthusiasm is implanted in Adam and his children, from the beginning to the end of the world. It is given to them and they are poisoned by the old dragon. It is the origin of the power and might of all the heresies, even that of the papacy and Mohammed. [10] Therefore we should and must insist that God does not want to deal with us human beings, except by means of his external word and sacrament. Everything that is attributed to the Spirit apart from such a word and sacrament is of the devil. [11]Also, God wanted to appear to Moses first in the burning bush and by means of the spoken word.[159] No prophet, neither Elijah nor Elisha, received the Spirit apart from or without the Ten Commandments. [12]John the Baptist was not conceived without Gabriel's preceding word,[160] and he did not leap in his mother's womb without Mary's voice.[161] [13]St. Peter says: the prophets did not prophesy "by human will" but "by the Holy Spirit" as "holy people of God."[162] Without the external word, they were not holy and much less would the Holy Spirit have moved them to speak while they were still unholy. Peter says they were holy when the Holy Spirit speaks through them.

[Article 9:] On Excommunication

We maintain that the "great" excommunication, as the pope calls it, is a purely secular penalty and does not touch us who are servants of the church. However, the "small" (that is, the truly Christian) excommunication is that we should not allow public, obstinate sinners to come to the sacrament or other assemblies of the church until they correct themselves and avoid sin. The preachers should not mix civil punishments together with this spiritual penalty or excommunication.[163]

158. Exod. 4:21; 7:13; 10:20; 11:10; 14:4.

159. Exod. 3:2ff.

160. Luke 1:13-20.

161. Luke 1:41-44.

162. 2 Peter 1:21.

163. The *excomunicatio major* excluded a person from both the church and political communities, while the *excommunicatio minor* restricted a person only from the sacrament. The biblical foundation for excommunication was found in Matt. 18:15ff.

[Article 10:] On Ordination and Vocation

[1]If the bishops want to be true bishops and embrace the church and the gospel, then, for the sake of love and unity (and not out of necessity), we might allow them to ordain and confirm us and our preachers—if all the pretense and fraud of unchristian ceremony and pomp are set aside. However, they are not and do not want to be true bishops. [2]Rather, they are political lords and princes who do not want to pay attention to preaching, teaching, baptizing, communing, or any proper work or office of the church. In addition, they drive out, persecute, and condemn those who are called to such an office. Still, the church must not remain without servants on their account.[164]

[3]Therefore, as the ancient examples of the church and the fathers teach us, we want to and should ourselves ordain suitable persons to such an office. They have not been able to forbid or prevent us, even in accordance with their own laws, because their laws say that those who are ordained by heretics should be regarded as ordained and remain ordained.[165] Similarly, St. Jerome wrote about the church at Alexandria that it had originally been ruled by the priests and preachers together, without bishops.[166]

[Article 11:] On the Marriage of Priests

[1]The bishops have forbidden marriage and burdened the godly estate of priests with perpetual celibacy—and they have had neither the authority nor the right. Rather, they have dealt with it like anti-Christian, tyrannical, wicked rascals. With this, they have given the occasion for all kinds of horrible, enormous, innumerable sins of unchastity. They are still stuck in these things. [2]Now, they have as much power to make a young woman out of a young man or to make a young man out of a young woman as they do to abolish sexual distinctions altogether. They have also had little power to separate or inhibit such creatures of God so that they should not honestly and conjugally live with one another. [3]Therefore we do not want to comply with their mis-

---

164. FCSD, 10, 19.

165. Gratian, *Decretum,* Part I, dist. 68, chap. 1; Part III, dist. 4, chap. 107. Cochläus writes: "Luther says too much when he says, 'those who are ordained by heretics should be regarded as ordained and remain ordained,' according to our papal laws. That only applies to those heretics who ordain according to the order and usage of the church, as the Arians, Donatists, Pelagians, etc., did. They used the churchly form of consecration. Their children, who were baptized by them need not be baptized again. Similarly, their priests and deacons, who were ordained by consecrated bishops, do not have to be reordained. However, Luther will never show, either from St. Jerome or from papal law, that we should consider the mockery of a bishop's ordination by Luther or Bugenhagen (performed without oil or charism, against the order of the Christian church and without properly ordained bishops in attendance) a real ordination" (*CC,* 48).

166. SA II, 4, 9.

erable singleness. We do not tolerate it. We maintain that marriage is free, as God ordered and founded it. We do not want to disrupt or inhibit God's work. St. Paul says it would be "a teaching of demons." [167]

[Article 12:] On the Church

[1]We do not acknowledge to them that they are the church, and they are not the church.[168] [2]We do not want to hear what they command or forbid in the name of the church, because, God be praised, a seven-year-old child[169] knows what the church is: holy believers and "little sheep who hear the voice of their shepherd." [170] [3]This is why children pray in this way, "I believe in one holy Christian church." [171] This holiness does not exist in surplices, shaved heads, long albs, and their other ceremonies they have devised over and above the Holy Scriptures. Its holiness exists in the word of God and true faith.

[Article 13:] On Being Justified before God and on Good Works[172]

[1]I have no idea how to change what I have consistently taught about this until now, namely, that we receive a different, new, clean heart through faith (as St. Peter says).[173] God wants to regard and does regard us as completely righteous and holy, for the sake of Christ our mediator. Although sin in the flesh is still not completely gone or dead, God will still not count it or consider it.

[2]After such faith, renewal, and forgiveness of sin, good works follow, and whatever in these works is still sinful or imperfect should not be even counted as sin or imperfection, for the sake of Christ. The human being should be called and should be completely righteous and holy, according to both the person and his or her works from the pure grace and mercy that have been poured and spread over us in Christ. [3]Therefore we cannot boast about the great merit of our works, where they are viewed without grace and mercy. Rather, as it is written, "Let the one who boasts, boast in the Lord." [174] [4]If

---

167. 1 Tim. 4:1.

168. Luther called the pope "a damned heretic and schismatic" in *D. M. Luthers Appellation an ein christlich frei Concilium verneuert,* 1520 (*WA* 7:89).

169. Seven was the earliest age of discernment (*WA* 51:524 n. 6).

170. John 10:3. FCSD 10, 19.

171. The Latin translation: "I believe in the holy Catholic or Christian church." Luther quotes from a German translation of the creed that had been in use in Germany since the fifteenth century. TCS I, 3; TCS II, 3; AC 6 and 7; SC II, 3; LC II, 3.

172. LC II, 47–50.

173. Acts 15:9.

174. 1 Cor. 1:31; 2 Cor. 10:17.

one has a gracious God, then everything is good. Furthermore, we say also that if good works do not follow, then the faith is false and not true.

[Article 14:] On Monastic Vows

[1]Because monastic vows are in direct conflict against the first and chief article, they should simply be done away with. Christ spoke in Matthew 24[:5] about those who say, "I am Christ," etc. [2]Those who vow to live a monastic life believe that they lead a better life than common Christians, and through their works intend to help not only themselves but others to get to heaven. [3]This is known as denying Christ, etc. They boast, on the basis of St. Thomas, that monastic vows are equal to baptism. This is blasphemy against God.[175]

[Article 15:] On Human Regulations

[1]The papists say that human regulations effect the forgiveness of sins or merit salvation. That is unchristian and damnable. As Christ says, "In vain do they worship me, teaching human precepts as doctrines."[176] Also, the letter to Titus [1:14]: "those who reject the truth." [2]Furthermore, it is not right when they say that it is a mortal sin to break such human regulations.[177]

[3]These are the articles on which I must stand and on which I intend to stand, God willing, until my death. I know of nothing in them that can be changed or conceded. If anyone does so, it is on that person's conscience.[178]

[4]Finally, the papal bag of tricks is still filled with foolish, childish things such as the consecration of churches, baptizing bells, baptizing altar stones, and inviting the donors who give money for these things to the rites. This baptizing is a mockery and an effrontery to Holy Baptism. We ought not tolerate it.

[5]Moreover, there is the consecration of candles, palms, spices, oats,

---

175. The last sentence of SA III, 14 was written into the text of the original manuscript by Luther himself, presumably when he reviewed his dictation of SA III, 4 to SA III, 15 (*UuA*, 68).

176. Matt. 15:9.

177. Cochläus writes, "Whoever breaks these traditions out of wickedness, with contempt for the priests and bishops, and leads the weak and simple into defiance and scandal (as Luther's followers do daily—eating meat and breaking fasts, etc.), without doubt commit a serious mortal sin" (*CC*, 57).

178. SA III, 15, 3 is out of place here. Perhaps Luther meant them to be part of an extended subscription, but these words were separated from his signature. Both the original 1538 publication of SA and the 1580 *Book of Concord* suggested a break in Luther's train of thought here when they began this paragraph with an ornamental initial.

cakes, etc.[179] Nevertheless, this cannot be called or be consecration. Rather, this is pure mockery and deception. For such innumerable magic tricks, we commend them to their God and to themselves until they become tired of them. We intend to be unmolested with these things.

Subscriptions to the Schmalkald Articles

Dr. Martin Luther subscribes

Dr. Justus Jonas, rector, subscribes with his own hand

Dr. John Bugenhagen, Pomeranian, subscribes

Dr. Caspar Cruciger subscribes

Nicholas Amsdorf of Magdeburg subscribes

George Spalatin of Altenburg subscribes

I, Philip Melanthon,[180] also regard the above articles as true and Christian. About the pope, however, I maintain that if he would allow the gospel, we might allow to him his superiority over the bishops which he has "by human right." We could make this concession for the sake of peace and general unity among those Christians who are now under him and might be in the future.

John Agricola of Eisleben subscribes[181]

Gabriel Didymus subscribes[182]

I, Dr. Urban Rhegius, superintendent of the churches in the Duchy of Lüneburg, subscribe for myself and in the name of my brothers and in the name of the church of Hanover

I, Stephen Agricola, as minister to the Elector, subscribe

And I, John Draconites, professor and minister of Marburg, subscribe

I, Conrad Figenbotz, subscribe to the glory of God that I have believed and I preach and I believe firmly as above

I, Andreas Osiander, minister of Nürnberg, subscribe

Master Veit Dietrich, minister of Nürnberg

---

179. On Holy Saturday, the "old fire" was extinguished in the church, the "new fire" was lit and sprinkled with holy water. At the Easter Vigil, the Easter candle was consecrated and lit from this "new fire." On Candlemass (February 2), candles were consecrated. On Palm Sunday, palms were consecrated. On the Assumption of Mary (August 15), herbs, flowers, ears of corn, honey, grape-vines, etc., were consecrated. On St. Stephen's Day (December 26), oats were consecrated. On Easter Sunday, unleavened Easter cakes were consecrated. *BSLK,* 462 n. 8.

180. Melanchthon began using "Melanthon" in 1531 (Heinz Scheible, "Luther and Melanchthon," *LQ* 4, 3 [Autumn 1990]: 330f.).

181. The first eight subscriptions to SA were obtained at a gathering of theologians at Wittenberg, in December 1536.

182. Didymus signed SA in January 1537.

I, Erhard Schnepf, preacher of Stuttgart, subscribe

Conrad Oettinger of Pforzheim, preacher of Duke Ulrich

Simon Schneeweiss, servant of the church in Crailsheim

I, John Schlagenhaufen, pastor of the church of Köthen, subscribe

Master George Helt of Forchheim

Master Adam of Fulda, preacher of Hesse

Master Anton Corvinus

I, John Bugenhagen, subscribe again, in the name of Master John Brenz, who, when leaving Schmalkalden, directed me to do both orally and in a letter, which was shown to these brothers who have subscribed [Luther's articles][183]

I, Dionysius Melander, subscribe to the Augsburg Confession, the Apology to the Augsburg Confession, and the Wittenberg Concord on the subject of the Eucharist

Paul Rhodius, superintendent of Stettin

Gerard Oemcken, superintendent of the church of Minden

I, Brixius Northanus, minister of the church of Christ which is at Soest, subscribe the articles of the Reverend Father Martin Luther and acknowledge that I have believed and taught likewise and, by the Spirit of Christ, will likewise believe and teach

Michael Caelius, preacher of Mansfeld, subscribes

Master Peter Geltner, preacher of Frankfurt, subscribes

Wendal Faber, pastor of Seeburg in Mansfeld

I, John Aepinus, subscribe[184]

---

183. Brenz's note to Bugenhagen reads: "I have read, and again and again, the Confession and Apology presented at Augsburg by the Most Illustrious Prince, the Elector of Saxony, and by the other princes and estates of the Roman Empire, to his Imperial Majesty. I have also read the Formula of Concord concerning the sacrament, made at Wittenberg with Dr. Bucer and others. I have also read the articles written at the Assembly at Schmalkalden in the German language by Dr. Martin Luther, our most revered preceptor, and the tract concerning the Papacy and the Power and Jurisdiction of Bishops. And, according to my mediocrity, I judge that all these agree with Holy Scripture, and with the belief of the true and lawful Catholic Church. But although in so great a number of most learned men who have now assembled at Schmalkalden I acknowledge that I am the least of all, yet as I am not permitted to await the end of the assembly, I ask you, most renowned man, Dr. John Bugenhagen, most revered Father in Christ, that your courtesy may add my name, if it be necessary, to all that I have above mentioned. For I testify in this my own handwriting that I thus hold, confess and constantly will teach, through Jesus Christ, our Lord. Done at Schmalkalden, Feb. 23, 1537" (*BSLK,* 466).

184. Aepinus (d. 1553) had originally subscribed SA thus: "John Apins of Hamburg subscribes. Concerning the superiority of the pontiff, we agree with all the representatives from Hamburg and assent to the sentences of Reverend Philip which were added at the end." He then reconsidered and signed without reservation (*UuA,* 126 [*WA* 50:254 n. 18]).

Likewise, I, John Amsterdam of Bremen

I, Fredrick Myconius, pastor of the church of Gotha in Thuringia, subscribe for myself and in the name of Justus Menius of Eisenach

I, John Lang, doctor and convener of the church of Erfurt, in my name and on behalf of my coworkers in the gospel, namely,[185]

The Rev. Licentiate Ludwig Platz of Melsungen

The Rev. Master Sigismund Kirchner

The Rev. Wolfgang Kiswetter

The Rev. Melchior Weittmann

The Rev. John Thall

The Rev. John Kilian

The Rev. Nicholas Faber

I, The Rev. Andrew Menser, subscribe in my own hand

And I, Egidius Melcher, have subscribed with my own hand

185. The final ten subscriptions were obtained in March 1537, when Luther and his entourage stopped in Erfurt on their way back to Wittenberg from Schmalkalden (*UuA*, 137 n. 1).

Names and Terms

Agricola, John (d. 1566). Teacher at the University of Wittenberg from 1519 (the same year he served as Luther's secretary at the Leipzig debate with John Eck). He began to speak publicly against the use of law in the church in the late 1520s. Agricola became a chief protagonist in the "antinomian controversy" at Wittenberg in the mid-1530s. He fell out of favor with both Melanchthon and Luther and went to Berlin as court preacher for the Elector of Bradenburg. He was the main Protestant architect of the Augsburg Interim.

All Saints' Day, November 1. Remembrance day for the dead, dating back to the tenth century. *WA* 30[II]:252, 260 n. 38; *Exhortation to All Clergy Assembled at Augsburg*, 1530 (*WA* 30[II]:351$_{20}$; *LW* 34:57).

Amsdorf, Nicolaus von (d. 1565). A student and, later, a professor at the University of Wittenberg. Von Amsdorf, a close friend of Luther, was with the reformer at Leipzig in 1519 and at Worms in 1521. Luther ordained him Bishop of Naumburg in 1543. After Luther's death, von Amsdorf saw himself as a defender of orthodox Lutheran teaching, most notably against George Major's assertion that "good works are necessary for salvation."

antichrist/anti-Christian (German: *Endechrist/lich*). In 1522 (Advent Postil, *WA* 10[I,2]:47), Luther had publicly expressed his dissatisfaction with *Endechrist* as the inherited, popular German translation of the Latin *Antichristus*. He preferred *Widerchrist*. In SA, however, Luther returned to *Endechrist* as all references to the antichrist, except in SA II, 4, 10. SA II, 2, 25; SA II, 4, 10, 14; SA III, 11, 1; *Brief Confession concerning the Holy Sacrament* (*LW* 38:310). Luther often pointed to the money matters of the Roman church as evidence of the anti-Christian nature of the papacy. E.g., *On the Papacy in Rome, Against the Most Celebrated Romanist in Leipzig*, 1520 (*WA* 6:289; *LW* 39:60); *To the Christian Nobility of the German Nation concerning the Reform of the Christian Estate*, 1520 (*WA* 6:416; *LW* 44:141); *Einer aus den hohen Artikeln des päpstlichen Glaubens*, 1537 (*WA* 50:80$_{17f.}$); *Luthers Vorrede über den Propheten Daniel*, 1541 (*WADB* 11[II]:100$_{10f.}$).

article(s). The traditional translation of *Artikel* into English, when used with respect to SA. This translation, although obvious and understandable, does not completely capture the force of what Luther is trying to communicate. The articles in the Lutheran confessional writings are not a series of encyclopedia or newspaper "articles" about the Christian faith. Other possible translations of *Artikel* are "basics," "things," "staples," "essentials," "properties," "goods," "inventory," etc. With this in mind, however, the traditional rendering of *Artikel* as "Article" is retained throughout the text.

Augustine of Hippo (d. 430). One of the most influential thinkers in Christian history. As bishop of the North African town of Hippo, Augustine synthesized Neoplatonic categories with the Scriptures and thus set the trajectory of Christian theology for at least the next thousand years. His most seminal works are *The City of God, The Confessions,* and *The Trinity.*

Bernard of Clairvaux (d. 1153). Abbot of the Cistercian monastery at Clairvaux, France, in the first half of the twelfth century. A noted preacher and hymn writer, Bernard played a decisive role in shaping the popular piety of his day.

Bugenhagen, John (d. 1558). A native of Wollin, Pomerania; sometimes referred to as Pomeranus or Pomer. He came to Wittenberg in 1521, and after a decade as pastor of the City Church, he began to lecture at the university, in the theological faculty. Bugenhagen collaborated with Luther in translating the Bible and contributed greatly to the organization of Protestant churches of northern Germany and Denmark.

bull, papal (German: *Bullen*). Papal decrees at the time were sealed with leaden fasteners (in Latin, *Bulla*) and were known popularly as "bulls." SA II, 4, 4.

Campegio, Lorenzo (d. 1539). Papal legate at the Diet of Augsburg in 1530.

canons, cathedral, and foundation (German: *Tumherrn*). Associations of secular priests and associations of women, connected to a cathedral or collegiate church. The women lived under a rule, but did not take perpetual vows as did nuns. The chapter schools were taught by the canons: men taught the boys and women taught the girls. See A. Werminghoff, *Verfassungsgeschichte der deutschen Kirche im Mittelalter* (2nd ed., 1913), 143–52, 190f. SA, Preface, 10.

chief- (German: *Häupt-/Haupt-*). A technical term that Luther uses regularly in SA. His various usages of this word (particularly the use of the prefix *Häupt*, in compounds) indicates a particular item of significance for Luther. *Häupt* is translated as "head" or "chief." ACAp IV, 2; SA, Preface, 13, 14; SA II, 2, 1, 7, 12, 25; SA II, 3, 2; SA II, 4, 3.

Cochläus, John (d. 1552). One of Luther's most ardent Roman Catholic controversialists. He wrote a point-by-point rebuttal to SA already in 1538. He referred to the numerous good reasons for the pope to postpone the council—not the least of which was the poor response by German prelates (*CC*, 61f.). See SA II, 4, 4.

Common Week, the. The seven-day period following St. Michael's Day (September 29) when numerous masses were said on behalf of the dead. *WA* 30^{II}:252, 260 n. 37; *Exhortation to All Clergy Assembled at Augsburg*, 1530 (*WA* 30^{II}:351$_{16}$; *LW* 34:56). See SA II, 2, 12.

Constance, Council of. A general council of the church, which met in the southern German city of Constance from 1414 to 1418. This council defined the sacramental doctrine of concomitance, burned John Hus at the stake, and ended the "great schism" of the Western church. SA III, 6, 2; *Vorrede zu Tres epistolae Ioannis Hussii*, 1536 (*WA* 50:16–19); *WATR* 3:3502, 3542; *Against the Roman Papacy, an Institution of the Devil*, 1545, (*WA* 54:208–10; *LW* 41:265–69).

correct(ly) (German: *gerecht/recht*). In SA, and more generally in both medieval and modern German, *Recht(en)*, as adjective, noun, and adverb, has a variety of meanings. Other possible translations are "right, righteousness, privilege, power, reason, dominance, justice, justify, law, claim, title, truth, legitimacy, authority, administration of justice," etc. See SA, Preface, 2, 10, 12; II, 1, 3; II, 4, 10, 14; III, 3, 2, 3, 9, 10, 12, 18, 27, 30, 32, 40, 42; III, 6, 5; III, 8, 4; III, 9; III, 10, 1, 3; III, 11, 1; III, 13, title, 1, 2, 4; III, 15, 2; Subscription #7.

Cruciger, Caspar (Creutziger) (d. 1548). Served as pastor of the Wittenberg castle church and professor of theology before becoming rector of the university in 1533. Cruciger assisted Luther in his translation of the Bible and participated in important theological debates and conferences. He took the ailing Luther's dictation of SA III, 4 to SA III, 11 and recorded many of Luther's famous "Table Talks." He was instrumental in reforming Leipzig in 1539, and he recorded Luther's dictation of SA III, 4.

Didymus, Gabriel (d. 1558). A former Augustinian monk who was pastor at the Electoral residence of Torgau; signed SA in January 1537. He was not present at Schmalkalden.

Dietrich, Veit (d. 1549). Was converted to Lutheranism in the early 1520s and became Luther's private secretary in 1527, accompanying the reformer to Marburg in 1529 and to the Coburg castle in 1530. Dietrich was a pastor in Nürnberg from 1535 until his death.

divine right, by (Latin: *jure divino*). A technical phrase in the medieval church used to underscore the divine institution and legitimacy of various church structures and practices. This phrase is used in distinction to "by human right" (*jure humano*). In *Disputatio I. Eccii et M. Lutheri Lipsiae habita*, 1519 (*WA* 2:279$_{23f.}$), Luther wrote about "the Holy Scriptures, which are properly the *jus divinum.*" SA II, 4, 1, 7, 13 and Melanchthon's subscription to SA.

dominance (German: *gerecht/recht*). In SA, and more generally in both medieval and modern German, *Recht(en),* as adjective, noun, and adverb, has a variety of meanings. Other possible translations are "right, correctness, righteousness, privilege, power, reason, justice, justify, law, claim, title, truth, legitimacy, authority, administration of justice," etc. SA, Preface, 2, 10, 12; II, 1, 3; II, 4, 10, 14; III, 3, 2, 3, 9.

Dominicans (German: *Predigermönchen*). Literally, the "preacher monks." The Dominicans are known as the Order of the Preachers. SA III, 5, 2.

enthusiasts (German: *Enthusiasten*). Luther tended to lump the so-called radical Reformation or left-wing Reformation together under such labels. Other favorite terms of derision Luther used to vilify these Protestant opponents were "fanatics" (German: *Schwärmer*) and "fanatical spirits" (German: *Rottengeister*). SA III, 3, 42; SA, II, 2, 11; III, 8, 3, 5, 9; Luther said this in his 1539 tract *On the Councils and the Church:* "Münzer called us Wittenberg theologians 'scholars of the book' (*Schriftgelehrten*) and himself a 'scholar of the spirit' (*Geistgelehrten*), and after him, many other follow his lead" (*WA* 50:646$_{33f.}$; *LW* 41:170); also, *Against the Heavenly Prophets in the Matter of Images and Sacraments,* 1525 (*WA* 18:136–39; *LW* 40:146–49); Luther's sermon on Pentecost, 1544 (*WA* 21:468f.); *Predigt am 2. Adventsonntag, nachmittags,* December 10, 1531 (*WA* 34^{II}:487$_{2f.}$); *Commentary on I Corinthians 15,* 1532 (*WA* 36:491, 499–506; *LW* 28:67, 75–82); *Freder, Dialogus dem Ehestand zu Ehren,* 1545 (*WA* 54:173$_{5-7}$); Letter from Luther to Spalatin, April 12, 1522 (*WABr* 2:493); Letter from Thomas Münzer to Luther, July 9, 1523 (*WA* 3:104–6); Letter from Luther to Spalatin, August 3, 1523 (*WABr* 3:120); Letter from Luther to John Briessmann, July 4, 1524 (*WABr* 3:315); *On War against the Turk,* 1529 (*WA* 30^{II}:107$_{18}$ [and n. 3]; *LW* 46:161). Heiko Oberman, *Luther: Man between God and the Devil* (New Haven: Yale University Press, 1989), 292.

estates (German: *Ständ(en)*). *See* orders (of creation).

excrement (German: *Geschmeiss*). See Luther's Sermon on Matthew 21:14ff., February 13, 1538 (*WA* 47:404$_{12}$) and *Brief Confession concerning the Holy Sacrament,* 1544 (*WA* 54:160$_{27}$; *LW* 38:310). SA II, 2, 11.

fanatical spirits (German: *Rottengeister*). Luther tended to lump the so-called radical Reformation or left-wing Reformation together under such labels. Other favorite terms of derision Luther used to vilify these Protestant opponents were "fanatics" (German: *Schwärmer*) and "enthusiasts" (German: *Enthusiasten*). SA II, 2, 11; SA III, 3, 42; SA III, 8, 5, 6, 9. *See* enthusiasts.

foolishness/foolish activities (German: *Närrenswerk/Narrenswerk*). SA, Preface, 13; SA II, 4, 14; SA III, 15, 4.

Franciscans (German: *Barfussenmönchen*). Literally, the "barefoot monks." The Order of Friars Minor was known for its vow of poverty that could include a prohibition on owning shoes. SA III, 5, 3.

fraternities (German: *Bruderschaften*). In the eighth century, monasteries began to form "societies" within themselves that were obligated to pray for and perform works of piety on behalf of deceased brothers. In the late medieval period, societies arose that were based in parishes (either groups of clergy, lay and clergy together, or groups of lay people), which were designed to fulfill religious obligations. Concerning Luther's opinion of these societies, cf. *The Blessed Sacrament of the Holy and True Body of Christ, and the Brotherhoods,* 1519 (*WA* 2:754–58; *LW* 35:67–73). Cf. also A. Werminghoff, *Verfassungsgeschichte der deutschen Kirche im Mittelalter* (2nd. ed., 1913), 149 n. 4. SA II, 2, 21.

Gerson, Jean (d. 1429). One of the most influential theologians in the ecclesiastical conflicts of the late 1300s and early 1400s. He was a moderate conciliarist whose meditative emphasis influenced medieval mysticism greatly. Gerson was highly valued by Luther, particularly in the reformer's earlier years. Luther refers to Gerson's *De laude scriptorum,* XI (*J. Gersonis opera omnia,* ed. M. Louis Ellies du Pin [1706], 2:702). SA, Preface, 6.

head- (German: *Häupt-/Haupt-*). *See* chief-.

hocus-pocus (German: *Gaukelei/Gäukelei*). A term used by Luther to mock various pious practices of the sixteenth-century Roman Catholic Church, which he considered rather superstitious. Other possible translations include "magic," "tricks," and "sleight-of-hand." SA, Preface, 14; SA III, 12, 3; SA III, 15, 4, 5. *WATR* 5:634$_{11\text{ff}}$; *WATR* 5:636$_{26\text{ff}}$; *On the Councils and the Church,* 1539 (*LW* 41:17).

horror (German: *Greuel*). Rather often used by Luther to describe the papacy and papal practices. It also has the sense of "abomination," "abhorrence," "disgust." SA II, 2, 16; SA II, 2, 17. Philipp Deitz, *Wörterbuch zu Dr. Martin Luthers Deutschen Schriften* (Hildesheim: Georg Olms Verlagsbuchhandlung, 1961), 1:165.

invention, human (German: *Menschenfundl[in]*). A compound word used by Luther to describe the Roman Catholic practices that may or may not be permissible, but because they are invented by human beings and not commanded by God, they are not necessary. SA II, 2, 2; II, 3, 2; II 4, 1.

John "the Steadfast" (d. 1532). Elector Prince of Saxony from 1525 to 1532. He played a pivotal role in lodging the evangelical "protest" at the second

Diet of Speyer. He signed the Augsburg Confession of 1530 and helped to influence his son toward the Lutheran cause.

John Fredrick "the Magnanimous" (d. 1554). Elector Prince of Saxony from 1532 to 1554, nephew of Fredrick the Wise and son of John the Steadfast. A committed and theologically aware Lutheran, John Fredrick commissioned Luther to write what was to become SA, in December of 1536. See SA, Preface, 1.

Jonas, Justus (d. 1555). An intimate friend and close collaborator with Luther. He was with Luther at Worms (1521); attended the wedding of Luther and Katherine von Bora and bore witness to the subsequent consummation of the marriage (1525); he was at Marburg (1529) and at Luther's death (1546), and he preached Luther's first funeral sermon at Eisleben. Jonas had considerable humanistic training, which he used to translate important Reformation works (e.g., Luther's *Bondage of the Will* and Melanchthon's *Loci*) from Latin into German. Jonas was dean of the theological faculty at Wittenberg for a decade (1523–33), lecturing on both the Old and the New Testament. As a church visitor in Saxony, he wrote the new church ordinances enacted there as a result of the Reformation.

jubilee year (German: *Guldenjahr*). Literally, "golden year" or "money year." In 1300, Boniface VIII published the bull *Antiquorum habet fida,* thus instituting a jubilee year, which promised a plenary indulgence for all who made a pilgrimage to Rome. Pope Sixtus IV established a papal indulgence for the dead in 1476. By 1500, indulgences for the dead were connected to the jubilee years. SA III, 3, 25, 26, 27.

justified (German: *gerecht/recht*). In SA, and more generally in both medieval and modern German, *Recht(en),* as adjective, noun, and adverb, has a variety of meanings. Other possible translations are "right, correctness, righteousness, privilege, power, reason, dominance, justice, law, claim, title, truth, legitimacy, authority, administration of justice," etc. SA, Preface 2, 10, 12; II, 1, 3.

law(s) (German: *Recht/recht*). In SA, and more generally in both medieval and modern German, *Recht(en),* as adjective, noun, and adverb, has a variety of meanings. Other possible translations are "right, correctness, righteousness, privilege, power, reason, dominance, justice, justify, law, claim, title, truth, authority, administration of justice," etc. SA, Preface, 2, 10, 12.

legitimacy (German: *Recht/recht*). In SA, and more generally in both medieval and modern German, *Recht(en),* as adjective, noun, and adverb, has a variety of meanings. Other possible translations are "right, correctness, righteousness, privilege, power, reason, dominance, justice, justify, law, claim, title, truth, authority, administration of justice," etc. SA, Preface, 2, 10, 12.

magic (German: *Gaukelei/Gäukelei*). A term used by Luther to mock various pious practices of the sixteenth-century Roman Catholic Church, which he considered rather superstitious. Other possible translations include "hocus-pocus," "tricks," and "sleight-of-hand." SA, Preface, 14; SA III, 12, 3; SA III, 15, 4, 5. *WATR* 5:634$_{11ff.}$; *WATR* 5:636$_{26ff.}$; *On the Councils and the Church*, 1539 (*LW* 41:17).

Massling (German: *Messeknecht*). Literally translated "mass-slave/servant." Cochläus says that the reformer invented this pejorative word to lampoon the theology of the priestly role in the celebration of the Mass (*CC,* 17). SA II, 2, 7, 10.

Melanchthon, Philip (d. 1560). An influential and important coworker with Luther in the Reformation. Master Philip (he never attained the doctorate) came to the University of Wittenberg in 1518 as an instructor in Greek. He wrote the first Lutheran dogmatics, the *Loci communes,* in 1521, which was revised and reprinted some eighty times in his lifetime. Melanchthon's participation in the establishment or reorganization of the Universities of Marburg, Königsberg, Jena, and Leipzig earned him the title *Praeceptor Germaniae* ("The Teacher of Germany").

Mohammed. The Muslim prophet (A.D. 570?–632). Luther's 1542 introduction to *Verlegung des Alcoran Bruder Richardi,* 1542 (*WA* 53:272$_{16-24}$). SA III, 8, 9.

Münzer, Thomas (d. 1525). Leader of a sixteenth-century revolutionary movement that sought to establish the reign of God on earth. Münzer was an early follower of Luther who broke with the reformer over differences regarding the relationship between politics and the gospel. Münzer, who occasionally referred to himself as "Martin's competitor for the affection of the Lord," became, in Luther's mind, the symbolic representation of all the radical or left-wing Reformation movements. Münzer was executed when his theocracy at Frankenhausen was overthrown in May 1525. Carter Lindberg, "Müntzeriana," *LQ* 4, 2 (Summer 1990): 195–214.

one form of the sacrament. This refers to the practice of distributing just the bread, and not the wine, to the congregation during the celebration of Mass. SA III, 6, 2.

opportunity (German: *Stätt und Raum haben*). Literally, this idiom could be translated "to have place and room." SA III, 2, 2.

orders (of creation) (German: *Ständ(en)*). Luther mentions three such created orders (or "estates") in SA: church, government, and home/economy. These created orders connote for the reformer the spheres of life in which one lives out one's vocation or calling. Although Luther numbered and labeled these "orders of creation" variously throughout his career, in SA the reformer tends to identify three basic categories: the church, the home (marriage/family and the economy), and the state (government). Christian participation in the *Ständen* is how the church influences the social arena, as Christians live out their vocation or calling. See the Latin epigram the reformer penned on the cover of his original monograph of SA; SA, Preface, 12, 13 14; II 3, 2; II, 4, 7; III, 11, 1.

papist (German: *Papist(en)*). A pejorative word used by Luther to describe someone who submits to papal authority (i.e., a Roman Catholic). Luther often described the church of Rome as "papal" (*papistische*) rather than "catholic" (*katholische*). SA III, 12, 3. *Sermons on the Gospel of John*, 1538 (*LW* 24:310), and Friedrich Heiler, *Urkirche und Ostkirche* (Munich: Verlag von Ernst Reinhardt, 1937), 9.

Paul III, Pope (d. 1549). Published the council bull *Ad dominici gregis curam*, on June 2, 1536 (*UuA*, 15). Pentecost in 1537 was on May 23. After numerous postponements and delays, the council met at Trent, from 1545 to 1565. See H. Jedin, *A History of the Council of Trent* (London: Thomas Nelson & Sons, 1957), 1:288ff. SA, Preface, 15, and the note in that place.

penance (German: *Busse*). *Busse* can also be translated "repentance." At some points in SA, Luther has in mind repentance as a faithful response to the recognition of one's sin. At other points, he has in mind penance as a liturgical, sacramental act. See Bernhard Lohse, "Beichte und Busse in der lutherischen Reformation," in *Lehrverurteilungen—kirchentrennend?* vol. 2: *Materialien zu den Lehrverurteilungen und zur Theologie der Rechtfertigung*, ed. Karl Lehmann (Göttingen: Vandenhoeck & Ruprecht, 1989), 283–95.

In its verbal forms, both the German (*Busse tun* or *büssen*) and the Latin (*poententiam agite*) can be translated into English as "repent" or "do penance." Luther had interpreted this phrase in the first thesis of *The Disputation on the Power and Efficacy of Indulgences* (the Ninety-five Theses), 1517 (*WA* 1:233–38; *LW* 31:19–33) as a call for the entire Christian life to be a life of repentance. This ambiguity is evident in the 1959 *Book of Concord*: Theodore Tappert translated the title of AC 12 as "Repentance," whereas Jaroslav Pelikan translated the title of ACAp 12 as "Penitence." SA III, 3.

pests, noxious (German: *Unziefers*). Should be seen in relation to Luther's well-known designation of the "enthusiasts" of the Reformation period as a "swarm" (*Schwärmerei*). SA II, 2, 11; SA III, 3, 42; III, 8, 4; and *Sermons on the Gospel of St. John* (*LW* 22:68).

Pomeranius, John. *See* Bugenhagen, John.

rascal/rascality (German: *Buben/Buberei*). SA II, 2, 1, 7, 16, 22; SA II, 4, 3; SA III, 3, 20; Letter from Justus Jonas to Luther, June 1530 (*WABr* 5:431); *A*

Treatise on the New Testament, that is the Holy Mass, 1520 (*LW* 35:102); *The Babylonian Captivity of the Church,* 1520 (*LW* 36:55, 56); and Thomas Aquinas (d. 1275), *Summa theologiae,* III, Question 64, Articles 5 and 9.

real(ly) (German: *gerecht/recht*). In SA, and more generally in both medieval and modern German, *Recht(en),* as adjective, noun, and adverb, has a variety of meanings. Other possible translations are "authority, right, administration of justice, righteousness, correctness, privilege, power, reason, dominance, justice, justify, law, claim, title, truth, legitimacy," etc. SA, Preface, 2, 10, 12.

remorse (German: *Reu*). Luther uses this word to translate the Latin word *contritio* ("contrition" or "remorse") into German. This was seen by the medieval church as the first step in "penance" (the second being "confession" and the third being "satisfaction"). Luther, however, thought that repentance had two parts: remorse and faith in the gospel of the forgiveness of sin. SA III, 3, 2, 12, 15–18, 27, 29, 36; SA III 3, 4.

repentance (German: *Busse*). *Busse* can also be translated "penance." At some points in SA, Luther has in mind repentance as a faithful response to the recognition of one's sin. At other points, he has in mind penance as a liturgical, sacramental act. See Bernhard Lohse, "Beichte und Busse in der lutherischen Reformation," in *Lehrverurteilungen—kirchentrennend?* vol. 2: *Materialien zu den Lehrverurteilungen und zur Theologie der Rechtfertigung,* ed. Karl Lehmann (Göttingen: Vandenhoeck & Ruprecht, 1989), 283–95.

In its verbal forms, both the German (*Busse tun* or *büssen*) and the Latin (*poententiam agite*) can be translated into English as "repent" or "do penance." Luther had interpreted this phrase in the first thesis of *The Disputation on the Power and Efficacy of Indulgences* (the Ninety-five Theses), 1517 (*WA* 1:233–38; *LW* 31:19–33) as a call for the entire Christian life to be a life of repentance. This ambiguity is evident in the 1959 *Book of Concord:* Theodore Tappert translated the title of AC 12 as "Repentance," whereas Jaroslav Pelikan translated the title of ACAp 12 as "Penitence." SA III, 3.

right/righteous/righteousness (German: *gerecht/recht*). In SA, and more generally in both medieval and modern German, *Recht(en),* as adjective, noun, and adverb, has a variety of meanings. Other possible translations are "correctness, privilege, power, reason, dominance, justice, jusitify, law, claim, title, truth, legitimacy, authority, administration of justice," etc. SA, Preface 2, 10, 12.

saved (German: *selig/seligerweise*). The root word *selig* is often related to the concept of salvation. Various forms of *selig* occur in SA and can be translated "save," "saved," "salvation," "salvific," etc. SA II, 4, 4, 12.

scholastic theologians (German: *Schultheologen*). Literally translated "school theologians." This word generally describes the Roman Catholic, university-based theologians of the late medieval church. Prominent among the school theologians were Albertus Magnus, Thomas Aquinas (d. 1275), and, later, John Duns Scotus (d. 1308). SA III, 1, 3; ACAp 2, 15; FCSD 2, 76.

sleight-of-hand (German: *Gaukelei/Gäukelei*). A term used by Luther to mock various pious practices of the sixteenth-century Roman Catholic Church, which he considered rather superstitious. Other possible translations include "hocus-pocus," "magic," and "tricks." SA, Preface, 14; SA III, 12, 3; SA III, 15, 4, 5. *WATR* 5:634₁₁ff.; *WATR* 5:636₂₆ff.; *On the Councils and the Church*, 1539 (*LW* 41:17).

sophist (German: *Sophist(en)*). A pejorative word, used by late medieval humanists to vilify scholastic theologians and their theological programs. Friedrich Lepp, *Schlagwörter des Reformationszeitalters* (Leipzig: M. Heinsius, 1908), 78–82. SA III, 3, 9; SA III, 6, 2, 5.

soul baths. Patrons founded free, public baths for the poor in order to demonstrate and enhance their (i.e., the donors') blessedness. *WA* 30^{II}:252, 260 n. 39; *Exhortation to All Clergy Assembled at Augsburg*, 1530 (*WA* 30^{II}:348₂₁; *LW* 34:54); *The Private Mass and the Consecration of Priests*, 1533 (*WA* 38:217₁₈; *LW* 38:173); *Matth. 18–24 in Predigten ausgelegt: Das dreiundzwanzigste Kapitel*, 1537–40 (*WA* 47:497₁₄). Gerhard Uhlhorn, *Die christliche Liebestätigkeit im Mittelalter* (Stuttgart, 1884), 2:310–13. SA II, 2, 12.

Spalatin, George (d. 1545). Luther's friend, court chaplain and private secretary to Fredrick the Wise and boyhood tutor of Elector John Fredrick. Spalatin served as secretary of a small meeting of evangelical theologians that had gathered to discuss what was to become SA in December of 1536. Spalatin made a copy of SA and delivered it to Elector John Fredrick in early January of 1537. Spalatin exercised great influence on behalf of the Reformation in the Saxon court.

spirituality (German: *Geisterei*). This word is related to Luther's rejection of what he calls "fanatical spirits" (German: *Rottengeister*). SA 8, 5.

superabundant works (German: *die ubrigen Verdienste*; Latin: *opera superabundantia* or *supererogationis*). The merits of the saints, or works of supererogation, were seen in the medieval period as those works that were performed by saints even after they had accumulated enough merit for themselves to gain entrance into heaven. The church, preeminently the pope, had the power to dispense these saints' "extra grace" or "extra merit," which were understood to accumulate in the church's "treasury of merit," to penitent sinners. SA II, 2, 24.

supererogation, works of. *See* superabundant works.

thunderclap (German: *Donneraxt*). Literally translated "thunder-axe." Luther uses this term to describe how the law, in its theological sense, works in a person's life. SA III, 2, 2.

transubstantiation (Latin: *transubstantio*). A theological explanation of how the sacrament works was established as dogma by Pope Innocent III at the Fourth Lateran Council in 1215. According to this theory, the "essence" or "substance" of the bread and the wine was changed into the real body and blood of Christ through the liturgical consecration of the priest. The outward, physical characteristics of the bread and the wine (the "nonsubstantial" or "nonessential" aspects of the elements—e.g., looks, taste, color), however, remained the same. SC VI. *The Blessed Sacrament of the Holy and True Body of Christ, and the Brotherhoods*, 1519 (*WA* 2:749; *LW* 35:59f.); *To the Christian Nobility of the German Nation concerning the Reform of the Christian Estate*, 1520 (*WA* 6:456; *LW* 44:198f.); *The Babylonian Captivity of the Church*, 1520 (*WA* 6:508–12; *LW* 36:28–35); *Contra Henricum Regem Angliae*, 1522 (*WA* 10^{II}:202–8); *Antwort deutsch auf König Heinrichs Buch*, 1522 (*WA* 10^{II}:245–49); *The Adoration of the Sacrament*, 1523 (*WA* 11:441; 36:287f.); *Confession concerning Christ's Supper*, 1528 (*WA* 26:437–45; *LW* 37:294–303); Letter from Luther to Prince George of Anhalt, May 25, 1541 (*WABr* 9:419); Letter from Luther to Prince John and Prince George of Anhalt, June 11 and 12, 1541 (*WABr* 9:443–45).

tricks (German: *Gaukelei/Gäukelei*). A term used by Luther to mock various pious practices of the sixteenth-century Roman Catholic Church, which he considered rather superstitious. Other possible translations include "hocus-pocus," "magic," and "sleight-of-hand." SA, Preface, 13, 14; SA III, 12, 3; SA III, 15, 4, 5. *WATR* 5:634$_{11ff.}$; *WATR* 5:636$_{26ff.}$; *On the Councils and the Church*, 1539 (*LW* 41:17).

true(ly) (German: *gerecht/recht*). In SA, and more generally in both medieval and modern German, *Recht(en)*, as adjective, noun, and adverb, has a variety of meanings. Other possible translations are "right, righteousness, correctness, privilege, power, reason, dominance, justice, justify, law, claim, title, legitimacy, authority, administration of justice," etc. SA, Preface, 2, 10, 12; II, 4, 10.

vicar (German: *Vikarist*). Low-ranking clergy who were attached to parish churches and served as representatives of the pastor. Vicars were also known as "chaplains" (German: *"Altarist"*). Cf. Georg Matthaei, *Die Vikariestiftungen der Lüneburger Stadtkirchen im Mittelalter und im Zeitalter der Reformation* (Göttingen, 1928). SA II, 2, 21.

Waim (or Wain), Gervasius of Memmingen. An ambassador of French King

Francis I, was in Saxony in 1531. Melanchthon once referred to him as "a most hostile enemy to our cause" (*CR* 2:517). *WABr* 2:31 n. 4; *WABr* 6:130 n. 1; Letter from Luther to Elector John Fredrick, February 9, 1537 (*WABr* 8:36$_{34-37}$); Letter from Luther to Justus Jonas, February 9, 1537 (*WABr* 8:39); *WATR* 6:4383. SA, Preface, 8.

Topical Index to Luther's Works and Lutheran Confessional Writings

ban, the. *See* excommunication.

baptism. AC 9; ACAp 9; SA III, 5; SC IV; LC IV; FCEp 12, 11–13. *A Sermon on the Estate of Marriage,* 1519 (*WA* 2:168; *LW* 44:9f.); *Eyn Sermon von dem heyligen Hochwirdigen Sacrament der Tauffe,* 1519 (*WA* 2:727–37); *The Babylonian Captivity of the Church,* 1520 (*WA* 6:526–38; *LW* 36:57–81); *The Order of Baptism,* 1523 (*WA* 12:42–48; *LW* 53:95–103); *Register über sämtliche Predigten* (*WA* 22:lxxxvif.); *Confession concerning Christ's Supper,* 1528 (*WA* 26:506; *LW* 37:367f.); *The Schwabach Articles,* 1529 (*WA* 30ᴵᴵᴵ:89; trans. in Michael Reu, ed., *The Augsburg Confession: A Collection of Sources with Historical Introduction* [Chicago: Wartburg Publishing House, 1930], 2:44f.); *Predigt am 2. Sonntag nach Epiphaniä,* January 18, 1534 (*WA* 37:258–67); *Predigt am Sonntag Septuagesimä,* February 1, 1534 (*WA* 37:270–75); *Predigten des Jahres 1534* (*WA* 37:627–72); *On the Councils and the Church,* 1539 (*WA* 50:630f.; *LW* 41:150f.); *Against Hanswurst,* 1541 (*WA* 51:487, 502; *LW* 41:199, 206f.).

baptism of children. LC IV, 47–57. Lectures on Galatians, 1519 (*WA* 2:507ff.; *LW* 27:246ff.); *The Babylonian Captivity of the Church,* 1520 (*WA* 6:538; *LW* 36:74f.); *WA* 11:301; *WA* 11:452; *WA* 17ᴵᴵ:78–88; *WA* 26:137f., 144–74; *The Schwabach Articles,* 1529 (*WA* 30ᴵᴵᴵ:89; trans. in Reu, *The Augsburg Confession,* 2:44f.); *The Marburg Articles,* 1529 (*WA* 30ᴵᴵᴵ:168f.; *LW* 38:88); Letter from Luther to Melanchthon, January 13, 1522 (*WABr* 2:425–27; *LW* 48:365–71); Letter from Luther to Spalatin, May 29, 1522 (*WABr* 2:546). Theodor Kolde, *Analecta Lutherana* (Gotha: Friedrich Andreas Perthes, 1883), 219f. The section "On Baptism" in WC.

bishops. SA II, 4, 1; Tr 13–17. *Disputatio I. Eccii et M. Lutheri Lipsiae habita,* 1519 (*WA* 2:261); *Contra malignum I. Eccii iudicium M. Lutheri defensio,* 1519 (*WA* 2:641f.); *Against the Roman Papacy, an Institution of the Devil,* 1545 (*WA* 54:243; *LW* 41:307f.); *On the Councils and the Church,* 1539 (*WA* 50:538f., 550, 576, 581; *LW* 41:41f., 56f., 88f., 93f.). SA III, 10, 1; *Exhortation to All Clergy Assembled at Augsburg,* 1530 (*WA* 30ᴵᴵ:340–43; *LW* 34:50–52); *The Private Mass and the Consecration of Priests,* 1533 (*WA* 38:195₁₇f.,

236$_{23ff.}$; *LW* 38:147, 194); *Predigt am Sonntag Exaudi,* May 9, 1535 (*WA* 41:241$_1$); *WATR* 4:4595.

blasphemy. AC 27, 11–14; ACAp 27, 20; SA II, 3, 2; SA II, 4, 3; SA III, 3, 43; SA III, 14, 3.

both forms, Communion in. AC 22; ACAp 22; SA III, 6 2–4. *The Blessed Sacrament of the Holy and True Body of Christ, and the Brotherhoods,* 1519 (*WA* 2:742f.; *LW* 35:49f.); *Verklärung etlicher Artikel in dem Sermon von dem heiligen Sakrament,* 1520 (*WA* 6:79–81); *Antwort auf die Zettel, so unter des Officials zu Stolpen Siegel ausgegangen,* 1520 (*WA* 6:137–40); *Ad schedulam inhibitionis sub nomine episc. Misnensis editam responsio,* 1520 (*WA* 6:144–51); *A Treatise on the New Testament, that is the Holy Mass,* 1520 (*WA* 6:374; *LW* 35:106f.); *To the Christian Nobility of the German Nation concerning the Reform of the Christian Estate,* 1520 (*WA* 6:456; *LW* 44:197f.); *The Babylonian Captivity of the Church,* 1520 (*WA* 6:498–500, 502–7; *LW* 36:12–16, 19–27); *Assertio omnium articulorum M. Lutheri per bullam Leonis X,* 1520 (*WA* 7:122–24); *Defense and Explanation of All Articles,* 1521 (*WA* 7:389–99; *LW* 32:55–62); *Receiving Both Kinds in the Sacrament,* 1522 (*WA* 10^{II}:20f., 24–29; *LW* 36:245f., 255); *Contra Henricum Regem Angliae,* 1522 (*WA* 10^{II}:201); *Antwort deutsch auf König Heinrichs Buch,* 1522 (*WA* 10^{II}:242); The Fifth Sermon, March 13, 1522, Friday after Inovcavit (*WA* 10^{III}:45f.; *LW* 51:90–91); *An Order of Mass and Communion for the Church at Wittenberg,* 1523 (*WA* 12:217; *LW* 53:34); *A Letter of Consolation to the Christians at Halle,* 1527 (*WA* 23:413–17; *LW* 43:151–56); *Ein Bericht an einen guten Freund,* 1528 (*WA* 26:564f., 590–614); *Exhortation to All Clergy Assembled at Augsburg,* 1530 (*WA* 30^{II}:320–23; *LW* 34:38–40); *Commentary on the Alleged Imperial Edict,* 1521 (*WA* 30^{III}:348–52; *LW* 34:80–82); *The Private Mass and the Consecration of Priests,* 1533 (*WA* 38:244–48; *LW* 38:204–9); *Sprüche wider das Konstanzer Konzil,* 1535 (*WA* 39^{I}:13–38); *Against Hanswurst,* 1541 (*WA* 51:490; *LW* 41:201); *Against the Thirty-Five Articles of the Louvain Theologians,* 1545 (*WA* 54:426, 432; *LW* 34:348–50, 355); Letter from Luther to Philip Melanchthon, August 1, 1521 (*WABr* 2:371f.; *LW* 48:277–82); Letter from Luther to John Hess in Oels, March 25, 1522 (*WABr* 2:482); Letter from Luther to George Spalatin, April 4, 1524 (*WABr* 3:265); Letter from Justus Jonas to Luther, June 30, 1530 (*WABr* 5:430; Letter from Luther to Justus Jonas, August 28, 1530 (*WABr* 5:593); Letter from Luther to Elector John, August 26, 1530 (*WABr* 5:572f.; *LW* 49:406–10); Letter from Luther to Lazarus Spengler, August 28, 1530 (*WABr* 5:590f.); Letter from Melanchthon to Luther, June 26, 1530 (*WABr* 5:397); Letter from Luther to George Spalatin, July 27, 1530 (*WABr* 5:502, 504f., 573f.; *CR* 2:208–14, 304, 349f., 354f.; *CR* 4:991–93, 1009–11.

ing the Forbidden Books of Dr. Martin Luther, 1521 (*WA* 7:297f.; *LW* 44:228f.); *Defense and Explanation of All Articles,* 1521 (*WA* 7:367–71; *LW* 32:42–47); *Von der Beicht, ob die der Babst macht habe zu gepieten,* 1521 (*WA* 8:138–85); *Receiving Both Kinds in the Sacrament,* 1522 (*WA* 10^{II}:32f.; *LW* 36:257f.); The Eighth Sermon, March 16, 1522 (*WA* 10^{III}:58–64; *LW* 51:97–100); *Predigt am Sonntag Lätare Nachmittags,* March 15, 1523 (*WA* 11:65); *An Order of Mass and Communion for the Church at Wittenberg,* 1523 (*WA* 12:216f.; *LW* 53:34f.); *Eyn Sermon am grunen donnerstag,* 1523 (*WA* 12:491–93); *Predigt am Palmsonntage,* March 20, 1524 (*WA* 15:481–89); *Predigt am Palmsonntag,* April 9, 1525 (*WA* 17^{I}:170f.); *Sermon von dem Sakrament,* 1526 (*WA* 19:513–23); *Confession concerning Christ's Supper,* 1528 (*WA* 26:507; *LW* 37:368f.); *Predigt am Gründonnerstag,* April 9, 1528 (*WA* 27:95–97); *Predigt am Palmsonntag,* March 21, 1529 (*WA* 29:136–46); *Exhortation to All Clergy Assembled at Augsburg,* 1530 (*WA* 30^{II}:287f.; *LW* 34:19f.); *The Schwabach Articles,* 1529 (*WA* 30^{III}:89; trans. in Reu, *The Augsburg Confession,* 2:43); *The Marburg Articles,* 1529 (*WA* 30^{III}:166f.; *LW* 38:87); *Sendschreiben an die zu Frankfurt a.M.,* 1533 (*WA* 30^{III}:565–70); Letter from Andreas Osiander to Luther, June 30, 1530 (*WABr* 5:433); Letter from Luther and Melanchthon to the Council of Nürnberg (*WABr* 6:454f.; *LW* 50:76f.; WC (*WABr* 12:21168–73). Kolde, *Analecta Lutherana,* 219.

creation. TCS I, 1; TCS II, 2; TCS III, 3, 4; AC 1, 1–4; SA I, 1; SC II; LC II, 9–24.

creeds. *See* **Holy Trinity.**

discipline. *See* **excommunication.**

ecclesiology. *See* **church, the.**

education. AC 27, 15–17; ACAp 27, 4–8; SA II, 3, 1. *To the Christian Nobility of the German Nation concerning the Reform of the Christian Estate,* 1520 (*WA* 6:439f., 452, 461; *LW* 44:173f., 191f., 205f.); *To the Councilmen of All Cities in Germany: That They Establish and Maintain Schools,* 1524 (*WA* 15:47; *LW* 45:370f.); *Confession concerning Christ's Supper,* 1528 (*WA* 26:504; *LW* 37:364); *Exhortation to All Clergy Assembled at Augsburg,* 1530 (*WA* 30^{II}:315–17; *LW* 34:36–38); *Einer aus den hohen Artikeln des päpstlichen Glaubens,* 1537 (*WA* 50:77f.); *On the Councils and the Church,* 1539 (*WA* 50:617, 651; *LW* 41:135, 176f.; *WATR* 4:675). See Martin Brecht's discussion of Luther's efforts in behalf of public education in the middle 1520s in *Martin Luther, vol. 2: Shaping and Defining the Reformation 1521–1532* (Minneapolis: Fortress Press, 1990), 141.

emperor, Holy Roman. SA II, 4, 16; Luther had referred to the emperor as "pious Charles, who is a sheep among wolves" (Letter from Luther to

Kaspar von Teutleben, June 19, 1530 [*WABr* 5:37330]); *Auf das Schreien etlicher Papisten über die siebenzehn Artikel*, 1530 (*WA* 30^{III}:196f.); *Dr. Martin Luther's Warning to His Dear German People*, 1531 (*WA* 30^{III}:291–98; *LW* 47:29–35); *Commentary on the Alleged Imperial Edict*, 1531 (*WA* 30^{III}:331f., 362, 388; *LW* 34:67f., 88, 104); Letter from Luther to Nikolaus Hausmann, July 6, 1530 (*WABr* 5:440; *LW* 49:348–52); *WATR* 2:1687, 2695.

empty effort/ritual. In 1520, Luther called the church of Rome a *Beth-aven*, a word borrowed from the Hebrew prophets (e.g., Hosea 4:15 and 10:5) that literally means "house of emptiness" (*The Babylonian Captivity of the Church* [*WA* 6:547; *LW* 36:88]). In his 1521 treatise, *The Misuse of the Mass*, Luther called the Wittenberg Castle Church (which housed the Elector's large and famous collection of relics) a *Beth-aven* (*WA* 8:561$_{21}$; *LW* 36:227). See also Isaiah 42:29; Zechariah 10:2; Habakkuk 1:3; *De abroganda missa privata Martini Lutheri sententia*, 1521 (*WA* 8:475$_{20}$); *The Misuse of the Mass*, 1521 (*WA* 8:556$_{22}$; *LW* 36:227); and Letter from Luther to George Spalatin, November 22, 1521 (*WABr* 2:405$_{14}$; *LW* 48:338). SA II, 3, 2.

Eucharist. *See* **Sacrament of the Altar.**

evil. *See* **sin.**

excommunication. AC 28, 8–21; ACAp 11, 4; ACAp 28, 13–14; SA III, 9; Tr 60, 74; FCEp 12, 26; FCSD 11, 89ff. *Explanations of the Disputation concerning the Value of Indulgences*, 1518 (*WA* 1:615–16; *LW* 31:228–30); *Sermo de virtute excommunicationis*, 1518 (*WA* 1:638–43); *A Sermon on the Ban*, 1520 (*WA* 6:63–75; *LW* 39:3–22); *Assertio omnium articulorum M. Lutheri per bullam Leonis X*, 1520 (*WA* 7:126f.); *Defense and Explanation of All Articles*, 1521 (*WA* 7:405–7; *LW* 32:65–67); *Matth. 18–24 in Predigten ausgelegt*, 1537–40 (*WA* 47:279ff. [esp. *WA* 47:282$_{23f.}$ and 284$_{22–26}$]); *Predigt am Sonntag Invokavit, nachmittags*, February 23, 1539 (*WA* 47:669–71); *WATR* 4, Nr. 4381. *Instructions for the Visitors of Parish Pastors in Electoral Saxony*, 1528 (*WA* 26:233–35; *LW* 40:311–13); *Predigt am 13. Sonntag nach Trinitatis, nachmittags*, August 22, 1529 (*WA* 29:539$_{1–3}$); Letter from Dionisius Binne to Luther, September 17, 1532 (*WABr* 6:360); Letter from Luther to Tilemann Schnabel and the other Hessen Clergy gathered at Homberg, June 26, 1533 (*WABr* 6:498$_{23f.}$); *WATR* 4:4073; *WATR* 5:5477. James Spalding, "Discipline as a Mark of the True Church in Its Sixteenth Century Lutheran Context," in *Piety, Politics, and Ethics: Reformation Studies in Honor of George Wolfgang Forell*, ed. Carter Lindberg (Kirksville, Mo.: Sixteenth Century Journal Publishers, 1984), 132.

filioque. TCS II, 3; TCS III, 22; SA I, 2.

good works. AC 6; AC 20; ACAp 4, 5–121; ACAp 20; SA III, 13; FCEp 3; FCSD 3. *Sermo de poenitentia*, 1518 (*WA* 1:324); *Heidelberg Disputation*,

1518 (*WA* 1:353, 356–59; *LW* 31:39f., 43–48); *Explanations of the Disputation concerning the Value of Indulgences*, 1518 (*WA* 1:593, 616; *LW* 31:189f., 230f.); *Luthers Unterricht auf etliche Artikel*, 1519 (*WA* 2:71f.); Lectures on Galatians 1–6, 1519 (*WA* 2:443–618; *LW* 27:151–410); *Disputatio de fide infusa et acquisita*, 1520 (*WA* 6:85f.); *Von den guten Werken*, 1520 (*WA* 6:202–76); *The Freedom of a Christian*, 1520 (*WA* 7:21–38, 50–73; *LW* 31:343–77); *Adversus armatum virum Cokleum*, 1523 (*WA* 11:298–302); *The Adoration of the Sacrament*, 1523 (*WA* 11:453; *LW* 36:300f.); *De loco Iustificationis*, 1530 (*WA* 30^{II}:657–76); *The Schwabach Articles*, 1529 (*WA* 30^{III}:88; trans. in Reu, *The Augsburg Confession*, 2:43f.); *The Marburg Colloquy and the Marburg Articles*, 1529 (*WA* 30^{III}:162–64, 166; *LW* 38:86–88); *The Disputation concerning Justification*, 1536 (*WA* 39^{I}:78–126; *LW* 34:145–96); *Die Promotionsdisputation von Palladius und Tilemann*, 1537 (*WA* 39^{I}:205 [see also XII and *WA* 39^{II}:426]); Lectures on Galatians, 1535 (*WA* 40^{I}:33—*WA* 40^{II}:184; *LW* 26:1–461—*LW* 27:1–144); *On the Councils and the Church*, 1539 (*WA* 50:597f.; *LW* 41:596ff.); Preface to the Epistle of St. Paul to the Romans, *WADB* 7:10$_{28ff.}$, 16$_{30ff.}$; *LW* 35:371, 374f.); Letter from Luther and Bugenhagen to Elector John Fredrick, May 10 or 11, 1541 (*WABr* 9:406–8); *Luther, Antwort auf schriftliche Fragen Melanchthons*, 1536 (*WABr* 12:189–95); *WATR* 6:6727.

gospel. AC 4; AC 5; ACAp 4; SA III, 4; FCEp 5; FCEp 6; FCSD 5; FCSD 6. *Sermo Dominica II. Adventus*, ca. 1514–17 (*WA* 1:105); *The Disputation on the Power and Efficacy of Indulgences* (the Ninety-five Theses), 1517 (*WA* 1:236$_{22f.}$; *LW* 31:31); *Explanations of the Ninety-Five Theses*, 1518 (*WA* 1:616f.; *LW* 31:230f.); *Ad librum eximii Magistri Nostri Magistri Amrosii Catharini, defensoris Silvestri Prieratis acerrimi, responsio*, 1521 (*WA* 7:720f.); *Adventspostille: Evangelium am 3. Adventssonntag*, 1522 (*WA* 10^{I,2}:158ff.); Sermons on the First Epistle of St. Peter, 1523 (*WA* 12:260; *LW* 30:3f.); *Ein Sendbrief des Herrn Wolfen von Salhausen an Doctor Martinus und Antwort Martin Luthers*, 1524 (*WA* 15:228); *Against the Heavenly Prophets in the Matter of Images and Sacraments*, 1525 (*WA* 18:65; *LW* 40:82); *Confession concerning Christ's Supper*, 1528 (*WA* 26:506; *LW* 37:366f.); *WA* 30^{III}:164f.; *The Schwabach Articles*, 1529 (*WA* 30^{III}:88; trans. in Reu, *The Augsburg Confession*, 2:44f.); *Preface to the New Testament*, 1546 (*WADB* 6:2–10; *LW* 35:357–62).

Holy Trinity. TCS I; TCS II; TCS III; AC 1; AC 3; ACAp 1; AC 3; SA I; SC II; LC I, 1; II; FCEp 8; FCSD 8. Cf. also *The Adoration of the Sacrament*, 1523 (*WA* 11:450$_{28-32}$; *LW* 36:298); *Confession concerning Christ's Supper*, 1528 (*WA* 26:500–502, 505; *LW* 37:361–63, 365f.); *The Schwabach Articles*, 1529 (*WA* 30^{III}:86f.; trans. in Reu, *The Augsburg Confession*, 2:40–44); *The Mar-*

burg Articles, 1529 (*WA* 30^{III}:160–62; *LW* 38:85f.); *Ein Bekenntnis christlicher Lehre und christlichen Glaubens,* 1530 (*WA* 30^{III}:178f.); *The Three Symbols or Creeds of the Christian Faith,* 1538 (*WA* 50:273–82; *LW* 34:215–29).

human regulations. AC 15; AC 26; AC 28, 29–78; ACAp 4, 233–43, 261–85; ACAp 4, 143–56; ACAp 7, 30–46; ACAp 15; ACAp 27, 14–37; SA III, 15; SC, Preface, 4–6; FCEp 10; FCSD 10. Cf. also *Confession concerning Christ's Supper,* 1528 (*WA* 26:509; *LW* 37:371f.); *The Schwabach Articles,* 1529 (*WA* 30^{III}:91; trans. in Reu, *The Augsburg Confession,* 2:45); *The Marburg Colloquy and the Marburg Articles,* 1529 (*WA* 30^{III}:168; *LW* 38:88).

incarnation. TCS I, 2; TCS II, 2; TCS III, 27; AC 3, 1–2; ACAp 3; SC II, 3–4; LC II; FCEp 8, 5, 11, 14, 15, 33; FCSD 8, 6, 24, 37, 71–73, 85.

indulgences. AC 25, 5; AC, Conclusion, 2; ACAp 12, 15, 98–105, 133–37, 175; ACAp 21, 23; SA II, 2, 24; SA III, 3, 24–27; Tr 45–48. Letter from Luther to Cardinal Albrecht, October 31, 1517 (*WABr* 1:111$_{21f.}$; *LW* 48:46). *Ex Sermone habito Domin. X. post Trinit.,* 1516 (*WA* 1:65–69); *Sermo de indulgentiis pridie Dedicationis* (*WA* 1:98f.); *Sermon on St. Matthew's Day,* February 24, 1517 (*WA* 1:141; *LW* 30f.); *The Disputation on the Power and Efficacy of Indulgences* (the Ninety-five Theses), 1517 (*WA* 1:233–38; *LW* 31:19–33); *Eynn Sermon von dem Ablasz unnd gnade durch den wirdigenn doctornn Martinum Luther Augustiner zu Wittenbergk,* 1517 (*WA* 1:243–46); *Eine Freiheit des Sermons päpstlichen Ablass und Gnade belangend,* 1518 (*WA* 1:383–93); Letter from Luther to John von Staupitz, May 30, 1518 (*WA* 1:525–27; *LW* 48:64–70); *Explanations of the Ninety-Five Theses,* 1518 (*WA* 1:527–628; *LW* 31:77–252); *Proceedings at Augsburg,* 1518 (*WA* 2:6–26; *LW* 31:253–92); *Appellatio a Caietano ad Papam,* 1518 (*WA* 2:28–30); *Luthers Unterricht auf etliche Artikel,* 1519 (*WA* 2:70); *Disputatio I. Eccii et M. Lutheri Lipsiae habita,* 1519 (*WA* 2:344–58); *The Babylonian Captivity of the Church,* 1520 (*WA* 6:497f.; *LW* 36:11f.); *Assertio omnium articulorum M. Lutheri per bullam Leonis X,* 1520 (*WA* 7:125f.); *Defense and Explanation of All Articles,* 1521 (*WA* 7:399–405; *LW* 32:62–66); *Papst Clemens VII zwei Bullen zum Jubeljahr,* 1525 (*WA* 18:255–69); *Confession concerning Christ's Supper,* 1528 (*WA* 26:507; *LW* 37:369); *Exhortation to All Clergy Assembled at Augsburg,* 1530 (*WA* 30^{II}:281–86; *LW* 34:16–18); *Bulla papae Pauli tertii de indulgentiis contra Turcam, etc.,* 1537 (*WA* 50:113–16); *Nachwort zu Johann Agricolas Übersetzung,* 1537 (*WA* 50:35$_{13f.}$); *Against Hanswurst,* 1541 (*WA* 51:488f.; *LW* 41:200); *WATR* 4:4153; *WABr* 1:111f.

Cochläus (cf. SA, Preface, 1 and the note in that place) responds to Luther: "Even though the guilt is forgiven by means of remorse and confession, sin must be punished through some works of penance: praying, fasting, vigils, pilgrimages, hard beds, hair-shirts, alms, etc., as has been done in the church for many hundreds of years" (*CC*, 27).

jubilee year(s). *To the Christian Nobility of the German Nation concerning the Reform of the Christian Estate,* 1520 (*WA* 6:437; *LW* 44:169f.); *Papst Clemens VII zwei Bullen zum Jubeljahr,* 1525 (*WA* 18:255–69); *Vermahnung an die Geistlichen, versammelt auf dem Reichstag zu Augsburg,* 1530 (*WA* 30ᴵᴵ:253); *Exhortation to All Clergy Assembled at Augsburg,* 1530 (*WA* 30ᴵᴵ:283; *LW* 34:16); *Einer aus den hohen Artikeln des päpstlichen Glaubens,* 1537 (*WA* 50:75f.); *Against the Roman Papacy, an Institution of the Devil,* 1545 (*WA* 54:268; *LW* 41:338f.); *Luthers Vorrede über den Propheten Daniel,* 1545 (*WADB* 11ᴵᴵ:86). Jubilee years were held in 1300, 1350, 1390, 1423, 1450, 1475, 1500, 1525.

justification. AC 2; AC 4; AC 6; 20; ACAp 4; SA II, 1; SA III, 4; SA III, 13; FCEp 3; FCEp 5; FCSD 3; FCSD 5.

keys, the. AC 25, 3–5; AC 28, 5–8; SA III, 7; ACAp 11, 2. Cf. also *Sermo in die Purificationis Mariae,* ca. 1514–17 (*WA* 1:131); *The Disputation on the Power and Efficacy of Indulgences* (the Ninety-five Theses), 1517 (*WA* 1:236₁₈f.; *LW* 31:31); *Explanations of the Disputation concerning the Value of Indulgences,* 1518 (*WA* 1:594–96, 615; *LW* 31:193–96, 228f.); *Proceedings at Augsburg,* 1518 (*WA* 2:11; *LW* 31:266f.); *Resolutio Lutheriana super propositione XIII. de potestate papae,* 1519 (*WA* 2:187–94); *Sermon Preached in the Castle at Leipzig on the Day of St. Peter and St. Paul,* June 29, 1519 (*WA* 2:248f.; *LW* 51:59f.); *The Sacrament of Penance,* 1519 (*WA* 2:722f.; *LW* 35:21); *On the Papacy in Rome, Against the Most Celebrated Romanist in Leipzig,* 1520 (*WA* 6:309; *LW* 39:86); *Concerning the Ministry,* 1523 (*WA* 12:183–85; *LW* 40:25f.); *The Keys,* 1530 (*WA* 30ᴵᴵ:435–507; *LW* 40:321–77); *Matth. 18–24 in Predigten ausgelegt,* 1537–40 (*WA* 47:288–97); *On the Councils and the Church,* 1539 (*WA* 50:631f.; *LW* 41:152f.); *Against the Roman Papacy, an Institution of the Devil,* 1545 (*WA* 54:249–52; *LW* 41:315–19).

law. ACAp 4; ACAp 5; ACAp 6; ACAp 12, 88–90; SA III, 2; FCEp 5; FCEp 6; FCSD 5; FCSD 6. Cf. also *WA* 1:398; *WA* 7:23f., 52f., 63f.; *WA* 8:609; *Kirchenpostille, Epistel am Neujahrstage, Galatians* 3:2–29, 1522 (*WA* 10ᴵ,¹:450–66); *Adventspostille: Evangelium am 3. Adventssonntag, Matthew* 11:2–20, 1522 (*WA* 10ᴵ,²:155–58); *Ein Sendbrief des Herrn Wolfen von Salhausen an Doctor Martinus und Antwort Martin Luthers,* 1524 (*WA* 15:228f.); *Against the Heavenly Prophets in the Matter of Images and Sacraments,* 1525 (*WA* 18:65; *LW* 40:82f.); *Theses concerning Faith and Law,* 1535 (*WA* 39ᴵ:50f.; *LW* 34:114ff.); *Die Tesen gegen die Antinomer,* 1537–40 (*WA* 39ᴵ:347); *Die zweite Disputation gegen die Antinomer,* 1538 (*WA* 39ᴵ:423–25); *Preface to the Epistle of St. Paul to the Romans,* 1546 (*WADB* 7:2–6,

12ff.; *LW* 35:365–69, 371ff.); Prefaces to the Old Testament, 1545 (*WADB* 8:16ff.; *LW* 35:238ff.).

marriage of priests. AC 23; ACAp 23; SA III, 11; Tr 78; LC I, 213–16. Cf. also *Contra malignum I. Ecci iudicium M. Lutheri defensio,* 1519 (*WA* 2:644); *Ad schedulam inhibitionis sub nomine episc. Misnensis editam responsio,* 1520 (*WA* 6:146); *On the Papacy in Rome, Against the Most Celebrated Romanist in Leipzig,* 1520 (*WA* 6:307f.; *LW* 39:83f.); *To the Christian Nobility of the German Nation concerning the Reform of the Christian Estate,* 1520 (*WA* 6:440–43; *LW* 44:175–79); *The Babylonian Captivity of the Church,* 1520 (*WA* 6:565; *LW* 36:114f.); *Answer to the Hyperchristian, Hyperspiritual and Hyperlearned Book by Goat Emser in Leipzig—Including Some Thoughts regarding His Companion, the Fool Murner,* 1521 (*WA* 7:674–78; *LW* 39:206–12); *Am dritten sontage ym Advent Epistell S. Pauli. I. Corinth. 4,* 1522 (*WA* 10^{1,2}:144f.); *Against the Spiritual Estate of the Pope and the Bishops Falsely So Called,* 1522 (*WA* 10^{II}:126–30, 149–53, 156f.; *LW* 39:266–68, 289–94, 297f.); *The Estate of Marriage,* 1522 (*WA* 10^{II}:279f.; *LW* 45:21f.); The Third Sermon, Tuesday after Invocavit, March 11, 1522 (*WA* 10^{III}:23–26; *LW* 51:79–81); *The Adoration of the Sacrament,* 1523 (*WA* 11:455; *LW* 36:303); 1 Corinthians 7 (*WA* 12:92–142; *LW* 28:1–56); *Exhortation to All Clergy Assembled at Augsburg,* 1530 (*WA* 30^{II}:323–40; *LW* 34:40–52); *Artikel wider die ganze Satanschule und alle Pforten der Hölle,* 1530 (*WA* 30^{II}:423, 426f.); *The Schwabach Articles,* 1529 (*WA* 30^{III}:90; trans. in Reu, *The Augsburg Confession,* 2:44); *Vorrede zu Confessio fidei ac religionis, etc.,* 1538 (*WA* 50:380); *On the Councils and the Church,* 1539 (*WA* 50:634–41; *LW* 41:156–64); Letter from Luther to Melanchthon, August 1, 1521 (*WABr* 2:370f.; *LW* 48:277f.); Letter from Luther to Melanchthon, August 3, 1521 (*WABr* 2:373f.; *LW* 48:283f.); Letter from Luther to Cardinal Albrecht, Archbishop of Mainz, December 1, 1521 (*WABr* 2:408; *LW* 48:342f.); Letter from Luther to Wenzeslaus Link, July 4, 1522 (*WABr* 2:575); Letter from Luther to Justus Jonas, June 30, 1530? (*WABr* 5:431); Letter from Luther to Lazarus Spengler, August 28, 1530 (*WABr* 5:593); Letter from Luther to the Brotherchurch in Mähren, November 5, 1536 (*WABr* 7:586).

Mass, the. AC 13; AC 21; AC 24; ACAp 13; ACAp 21; ACAp 24; SA II, 2; FCEp 7, 21ff.; FCSD 7, 108ff. Cf. also *A Treatise on the New Testament, that is the Holy Mass,* 1520 (*WA* 6:353–78; *LW* 35:75–111); *To the Christian Nobility of the German Nation concerning the Reform of the Christian Estate,* 1520 (*LW* 44:191f.; *WA* 6:451f.); *The Babylonian Captivity of the Church,* 1520 (*WA* 6:512–26; *LW* 36:35–57); *De abroganda missa privata Martini Lutheri sententia,* 1521 (*WA* 8:411–76); *The Misuse of the Mass,* 1521 (*WA* 8:482–563; *LW* 36:127–230); *Receiving Both Kinds in the Sacrament,* 1522 (*WA*

10^{II}:29; *LW* 36:254); *Contra Henricum Regem Angliae*, 1522 (*WA* 10^{II}:208–20; *Antwort deutsch auf König Heinrichs Buch*, 1522 (*WA* 10^{II}:249– 58); The Second Sermon, Monday after Invocavit, March 10, 1522 (*WA* 10^{III}:14–18; *LW* 51:75–78); *The Adoration of the Sacrament*, 1523 (*WA* 11:441f.; *LW* 36:287f.); *The Abomination of the Secret Mass*, 1525 (*WA* 18:22–36; *LW* 36:307–28); *WA* 26:508; *WA* 30^{II}:293–309, 610–15; *WA* 30^{III}:90f., 310f.; *WA* 38:195ff., 262–72; *WA* 39^{I}:139–73; Letter from Luther to Melanchthon, August 1, 1521 (*WABr* 2:37273; *LW* 48:281); *Luther an Propst, Dekan und kanoniker des Allerheiligenstifts zu Wittenberg*, August 19, 1523 (*WABr* 3:130–32); *An Order of the Mass and Communion for the Church at Wittenberg*, 1523 (*WA* 12:205–20; *LW* 53:15–40) and *The German Mass and Order of Service*, 1526 (*WA* 19:72–113; *LW* 53:51–90); *Confession concerning Christ's Supper*, 1528 (*LW* 37:316f.); Letter from Luther to Spalatin, July 27, 1530 (*WABr* 5:504f.); *Exhortation to All Clergy Assembled at Augsburg*, 1530 (*LW* 34:22f.); *Dr. Martin Luther's Warning to His Dear German People*, 1531 (*LW* 47:43f.). Luther referred to the Mass and celibacy as "the two pillars upon which the papacy rests": *A Letter of Dr. Martin Luther concerning His Book on the Private Mass*, 1534 (*WA* $38:271_{37}$; *LW* 38:233); *Contra Henricum Regem Angliae*, 1522 (*WA* $10^{II}:220_{13-16}$); *WATR* 1:113, 662, 1141; *WATR* 3:2852, 3319; *WATR* 5:6046.

masses, abuses of. *The Disputation on the Power and Efficacy of Indulgences* (the Ninety-five Theses), 1517 (*WA* $1:234_{33f.}$; *LW* 31:28); *The Babylonian Captivity of the Church*, 1520 (*LW* 36:35f.); *De abroganda missa privata Martini Lutheri sententia*, 1521 (*WA* 8:452–54); *The Misuse of the Mass*, 1521 (*WA* 8:531–33; *LW* 35:190–98); *Kirchenpostille: Evangelium am Tage der Heiligen drei Könige, Matth. 2:1-12*, 1522 (*WA* $10^{I,II}$:585–87); *Against the Spiritual Estate of the Pope and the Bishops Falsely So Called*, 1522 (*WA* $10^{II}:153_{8-10}$; *LW* 39:293f.); *Vorrede zu Menius, Der Wiedertäufer Lehre*, 1530 (*WA* 30^{II}:211); *Excurs* to *Exhortation to All Clergy Assembled at Augsburg* (*WA* 30^{II}:254); *Exhortation to All Clergy Assembled at Augsburg*, 1530 (*WA* $30^{II}:347_{28}$; *LW* 34:54f.); *Widerruf vom Fegefeuer*, 1530 (*WA* 30^{II}:385); *Dr. Martin Luther's Warning to His Dear German People*, 1531 (*WA* 30^{III}:310f.; *LW* 47:43f.); *Predigten des Jahres 1531*, Nr. 58, June 18 (*WA* $34^{I}:534_{f.}$); *Predigten des Jahres 1539*, Nr. 35, September 29 (*WA* $47:857_{8-15}$); *WATR* 3:3695.

masses for the dead. SA II, 2, 12. Commemorations held a year after a person's death are noted by the early church fathers: Tertullian (d. A.D. 220) in chapter 3 of *De corona* (MSL 2, 79). Ambrose of Milan (d. 397) mentions commemorations on the week and month after death in chapter 3 of *De obitu Theodosii oratio* (MSL 16, 1386). *Eine Freiheit des Sermons päpstlichen Ablass und Gnade belangend*, 1518 (*WA* $1:389_{35}$); *A Treatise on the New Tes-*

papae, 1519 (*WA* 2:183, 225, 236); *Sermon Preached in the Castle at Leipzig on the Day of St. Peter and St. Paul,* Matthew 16:13-19, June 29, 1519 (*WA* 2:248; *LW* 51:59); Letter from Luther to Hieronymus Dungersheim, December 1519 (*WABr* 1:567); Letter from Luther to Hieronymus Dungersheim, December 1519 (*WABr* 1:601–3); Letter from Justus Jonas to Luther (*WABr* 5:432); *Disputatio I. Eccii et M. Lutheri Lipsiae habita,* 1519 (*WA* 2:255, 258, 264); *Resolutiones Lutherianae super propositionibus suis Lipsiae disputatis,* 1519 (*WA* 2:397f., 432–35); *Contra malignum I. Eccii iudicium M. Lutheri defensio,* 1519 (*WA* 2:628–42); *On the Papacy in Rome, Against the Most Celebrated Romanist in Leipzig,* 1520 (*WA* 6:285, 287; *LW* 39:49, 57f.); *Epitoma responsionis ad Martin Luther,* 1520 (*WA* 6:328–48); *To the Christian Nobility of the German Nation concerning the Reform of the Christian Estate,* 1520 (*WA* 6:425f., 435; *LW* 44:152f., 166); *The Babylonian Captivity of the Church,* 1520 (*WA* 6:497f.; *LW* 36:11f.); *Assertio omnium articulorum M. Lutheri per bullam Leonis X,* 1520 (*WA* 7:127–31); *Warum des Papstes und seiner Jünger Bücher von D. Martin Luther verbrannt sind,* 1520 (*WA* 7:176); *Answer to the Hyperchristian, Hyperspiritual and Hyperlearned Book by Goat Emser in Leipzig—Including Some Thoughts regarding His Companion, the Fool Murner,* 1521 (*WA* $7:630_{34}$–631_3; *LW* 39:153–55); *Passional Christi und Antichristi,* 1521 (*WA* 9:703); *Defense and Explanation of All Articles,* 1521 (*WA* 7:409, 411; *LW* 32:68f.); *Ad librum eximii Magistri Nostri Magistri Ambrosii Catharini, defensoris Silvestri Prieratis acerrimi, responsio,* 1521 (*WA* 7:705–78); *Contra Henricum Regem Angliae,* 1522 (*WA* 10^{II}:197); *Antwort deutsch auf König Heinrichs Buch,* 1522 (*WA* 10^{II}:241); *Confession concerning Christ's Supper,* 1528 (*WA* 26:506; *LW* 37:366f.); *Concerning Rebaptism,* 1528 (*WA* 26:152f.; *LW* 40:237f.); Letter from Justus Jonas to Luther, June, 1530 (*WABr* 5:432); *The Keys,* 1530 (*WA* 30^{II}: 488; *LW* 40:353f.); *Vorrede zu R. Barns, Vitae Romanorum pontificum,* 1536 (*WA* 50:4); *Einer aus den hohen Artikeln des päpstlichen Glaubens,* 1537 (*WA* 50:78, 83, 84, $86_{15–22}$, 87); *Epistola Sancti Hieronymi ad Evagrium de potestate papae,* 1538 (*WA* 50:341–43); *The Three Symbols or Creeds of the Christian Faith,* 1538 (*WA* 50:269; *LW* 34:210f.); *On the Councils and the Church,* 1539 (*WA* 50:578; *LW* 41:90); *Luthers Vorrede über den Propheten Daniel,* 1545 (*WADB* 11^{II}:528f.); *Against the Roman Papacy, an Institution of the Devil,* 1545 (*WA* 54:209, 227, 229f., 235, 236, 243; *LW* 41:266, 288, 291f., 298, 307f.).

penance. Peter Lombard (d. 1160) taught a threefold understanding of penance (*contritio cordis, confessio oris, satisfactio operis*). *Sermo de indulgentiis pridie Dedicationis,* ca. 1514–17 (*WA* 1:98); Lectures on Romans, 1515 (*WA* 56:311–13; *LW* 25:298–300); Lectures on Romans, 1515 (*WA* 56:1; *WA*

und zu gemessen Wuerden (*WA* 2:70); *Disputatio I. Eccii et M. Lutheri Lipsiae habita,* 1519 (*WA* 2:322–44); *Defense and Explanation of All Articles,* 1521 (*WA* 7:451–55; *LW* 32:95–97); *De abroganda missa privata Martini Lutheri sententia,* 1521 (*WA* 8:452ff.); *The Misuse of the Mass,* 1521 (*WA* 8:531, *LW* 36:190f.); *Kirchenpostille: Evangelium am Tage der heiligen drei Könige (Matth. 2:1-12),* 1522 (*WA* 10^{II}:588f.); *The Adoration of the Sacrament* (*WA* 11:451; *LW* 36:299; *Sermon auf das Evangelium Luc. 16. Von dem reichen Manne und dem armen Lazarus,* June 7, 1523 (*WA* 12:596); *Confession concerning Christ's Supper,* 1528 (*WA* 26:508; *LW* 37:369f.); *Widerruf vom Fegefeuer,* 1530 (*WA* 30^{II}:367–90); *Dr. Martin Luther's Warning to His Dear German People,* 1531 (*WA* 30^{III}:309; *LW* 47:41f.); Letter from Luther to George Spalatin, November 7, 1519 (*WABr* 1:553); Letter from Luther to Nicholas von Amsdorf, January 13, 1522 (*WABr* 2:422; *LW* 48:362f.); *WATR* 3, Nr. 3695.

real presence. AC 10, 12; ACAp 10, 12; SA II, 2; SA III, 6; SC V; LC IV, 54–55; LC V; FCEp 7; FCSD 7. *Against the Heavenly Prophets in the Matter of Images and Sacraments,* 1525 (*WA* 18:170–75; *LW* 40:180–85); *That These Words of Christ, "This is My Body" Still Stand Firm against the Fanatics,* 1527 (*WA* 23:251; *LW* 37:130); *Confession concerning Christ's Supper,* 1528 (*WA* 26:506; *LW* 37:367f.); Letter from Luther to Martin Bucer, January 22, 1531 (*WABr* 6:25; *LW* 50:6f.); Letter from Luther to the Evangelicals in Venice, Vicenza, Treviso, June 13, 1543 (*WABr* 10:331).

rebaptism. *Concerning Rebaptism,* 1528 (*WA* 26:154–66; *LW* 40:239–54).

relics. SA II, 2, 22; LC I, 91; *Excurs* to *Exhortation to All Clergy Assembled at Augsburg,* 1530 (*WA* 30^{II}:254, 265f.); *Exhortation to All Clergy Assembled at Augsburg,* 1530 (*WA* 30^{II}:297$_{18}$, 298$_{17ff.}$, 348$_{29}$; *LW* 47:25, 27, 54); *Dr. Martin Luther's Warning to His Dear German People,* 1531 (*WA* 30^{III}:315$_{24ff.}$; *LW* 47:50); *The Last Sermon, Preached in Eisleben,* February 15, 1546 (*WA* 51:193$_{15f.}$; *LW* 51:390f.); *Neue Zeitung vom Rhein,* 1542 (*WA* 53:404f.); *WATR* 2:1272, 2399, 2638; *WATR* 3:3637b, 3785, 3867; *WATR* 4:4391, 4721, 4921, 4925; *WATR* 5:5484, 5844, 5853, 6466, 6469.

remorse, penitential. *Sermo de poenitentia,* 1518 (*WA* 1:319–22); *Decem praecepta Wittenbergensi praedicata populo,* 1518 (*WA* 1:446); *The Babylonian Captivity of the Church,* 1520 (*WA* 6:544f.; *LW* 36:84); *Assertio omnium articulorum M. Lutheri per bullam Leonis X,* 1520 (*WA* 7:113–17); *Defense and Explanation of All Articles,* 1521 (*WA* 7:355–67; *LW* 32:34–38).

repentance. AC 12; ACAp 12; SA III, 3; LC IV, 77–88; FCSD 5, 7ff. *Lectures on Romans,* 1515 (*WA* 56:311–13; *LW* 25:298–300); *Lectures on Romans,* 1515 (*WA* 56:1; *WA* 57:5; *LW* 25:3); Pauck, *Luther: Lectures on Romans,* 3; *Sermo de indulgentiis pridie Dedicationis,* ca. 1514–17 (*WA* 1:98f.); *The Disputa-*

Confession, 2:44f.); *The Marburg Colloquy and the Marburg Articles,* 1529 (*WA* 30^{III}:110–59, 169f.; *LW* 38:15–85, 88f.); *Sendschreiben an die zu Frank-furt a.M.,* 1533 (*WA* 30^{III}:558–65); *Glossae D. Martini Lutheri super senten-tias patrum,* 1534 (*WA* 38:298f.); *On the Councils and the Church,* 1539 (*WA* 50:631; *LW* 41:152); *Brief Confession concerning the Holy Sacrament,* 1544 (*WA* 54:161–67; *LW* 38:311); *Against the Thirty-Two Articles of the Louvain Theologians,* 1545 (*WA* 54:426; *LW* 34:354f.); *Letzte Streitschrift (contra asinos Parisienses Lovaniensesque),* 1545/46 (*WA* 54:452).

saints. ACAp 22, 32–34; SA II, 2, 25–28; LC I, 11. Luther's *Fourteen Consola-tions,* 1519–20, which was revised by Luther and reissued in 1536 (*WA* 6:99–134; *LW* 42:117–66); *Quaestio de viribus et voluntate hominis sine gra-tia disputata,* 1516 (*WA* 1:150); *Decem praecepta Wittenbergensi praedicata populo,* 1518 (*WA* 1:412–16); Letter from Luther to George Spalatin, De-cember 31, 1516 (*WABr* 1, 82f.).

satisfaction, penitential. ACAp 12, 13–16, 24. Cf. also *Ex Sermone habito Domin. X. post Trinit.,* 1516 (*WA* 1:65–69); *Sermo de indulgentiis pridie Dedicationis,* ca. 1514–17 (*WA* 1:98); *The Disputation on the Power and Efficacy of Indulgences* (the Ninety-five Theses), 1517 (*WA* 1:233; *LW* 31:25f.); *Ein Sermon von Ablass und Gnade,* 1517 (*WA* 1:243f.); *Sermo de poenitentia,* 1518 (*WA* 1:324); *Eine Freiheit des Sermons päpstlichen Ablass und Gnade belangend,* 1518 (*WA* 1:383–86); *The Babylonian Captivity of the Church,* 1520 (*WA* 6:548f.; *LW* 36:89f.); *Adversus execrabilem Antichristi bullam,* 1520 (*WA* 6:610); *Wider die Bulle des Endechrists,* 1520 (*WA* 6:624f.); *Against Hanswurst,* 1541 (*WA* 51:487f.; *LW* 41:199f.).

schools. *See* **education.**

sin. AC 2; AC 18; AC 19; ACAp 2; ACAp 18; SA III, 1; FCEp 1; FCEp 2; FCSD 1. *Lectures on Romans,* 1515 (*WA* 56:51ff., 309f.; 311–13; *LW* 25:44ff., 298–300); Lectures on Romans, 1515 (*WA* 56:1; *WA* 57:5; *LW* 25:3; Pauck, *Lu-ther: Lectures on Romans,* 3). *Sermo in Die sancti Matthaei,* ca. 1514–17 (*WA* 1:86); *Sermo Die Circumcisionis,* ca. 1514–17 (*WA* 1:121); *Quaestio de viribus et voluntate homininis sine gratia disputata,* 1516 (*WA* 1:145ff.); *Disputation against Scholastic Theology,* 1517 (*WA* 1:224; *LW* 31:9f.); *Sermo de poenitentia,* 1518 (*WA* 1:324); *Explanations of the Disputation concerning the Value of Indulgences,* 1518 (*WA* 1:544; *LW* 31:105f.); *Heidelberg Disputa-tion,* 1518 (*WA* 1:354; 359f.; *LW* 31:40f., 47ff.); *The Leipzig Debate,* 1519 (*WA* 2:161; *LW* 31:318); *Sermon Preached in the Castle at Leipzig on the Day of St. Peter and St. Paul,* Matthew 16:13-19, June 29, 1519 (*WA* 2:246f.; *LW* 51:56f.); *Ein Sermon gepredigt zu Leipzig auf dem Schloss am Tage Petri und Pauli,* 1519 (*WA* 2:424–26); *Assertio omnium articulorum M. Lutheri per bullam Leonis X,* 1520 (*WA* 7:142–49); *Adversus execrabilem Antichristi bul-*

lam, 1520 (*WA* 6:608); *Wider die Bulle des Endechrists,* 1520 (*WA* 6:622); *Defense and Explanation of All Articles,* 1521 (*WA* 7:445–51; *LW* 32:92–94); *Adventspostille,* 1522 (*WA* 10^{1,2}:28$_{20–26}$; *Fastenpostille,* 1525 (*WA* 17^{II}:80); *The Bondage of the Will,* 1525 (*WA* 18:600–787; *LW* 33:3–295); *Confession concerning Christ's Supper,* 1528 (*WA* 26:502f.; *LW* 37:362f.); *The Schwabach Articles,* 1529 (*WA* 30^{III}:87f.; *The Marburg Articles,* 1529 (*WA* 30^{III}:162f.; *LW* 38:85f.); *Commentary on the Alleged Imperial Edict,* 1531 (*WA* 30^{III}:359–64; *LW* 34:87–89); *Commentary on Psalm 50,* 1532 (1538) (*WA* 40^{II}:383f.: *LW* 12:350f.); *The Disputation concerning Justification,* 1536 (*WA* 39^{I}:84, 110–18; *LW* 34:153f., 179–87); *Commentary on Psalm 51,* 1538 (*WA* 40^{II}:322–25; *LW* 12:308–10); Thomas Aquinas, *Summa theologiae,* II, 1, Question 82, Article 3.

tradition. *See* **human regulations.**

vocation. *See* **ordination.**

vows, monastic. AC 27, ACAp 27; SA II, 3; SA III, 3, 28; SA III, 14. Cf. also *WA* 2:735f.; *WA* 6:440, 538–42; *WA* 7:625; *WA* 8:323–35; *Judgment of Martin Luther on Monastic Vows,* 1521 (*WA* 8:577–669; *LW* 44:243–400); *Kirchenpostille 1522, Gal. 3:23-29,* New Year's Day (*WA* 10^{1,1}:481–98); *The Gospel for the Festival of the Epiphany, Matthew 2:1-12,* 1522 (*WA* 10^{1,1}:681–709; *LW* 52:250–74); *An Answer to Several Questions on Monastic Vows,* 1526 (*WA* 19:287–93; *LW* 46:139–54); Letter from Luther to Philip Melanchthon, August 1, 1521 (*WABr* 2:370f.; *LW* 48:277–82); Letter from Luther to Philip Melanchthon, August 3, 1521 (*WABr* 2:374f.; *LW* 48:284f.); Letter from Luther to Philip Melanchthon, September 9, 1521 (*WABr* 2:382–85; *LW* 48:296–304); *To the Christian Nobility of the German Nation concerning the Reform of the Christian Estate,* 1520 (*WA* 6:440$_{5f.}$; *LW* 44:174); *The Babylonian Captivity of the Church,* 1520 (*WA* 6:539$_{16–19}$; *LW* 36:75f.); Lectures on Deuteronomy, 1525 (*WA* 14:624–26; *LW* 9:83f.); Lectures on Isaiah, 1527–29 (*WA* 25:186$_{22–25}$; *LW* 16:227f.); *Exhortation to All Clergy Assembled at Augsburg,* 1530 (*WA* 30^{II}:300$_{26–28}$; *LW* 34:27f.); *Predigt am 2. Sonntag nach Epiphaniä,* January 15, 1531 (*WA* 34^{I}:92$_{4f.}$); *Kleine Antwort,* 1533 (*WA* 38:148–58); *The Private Mass and the Consecration of Priests,* 1533 (*WA* 38:226$_{11}$f.; *LW* 38:183); *WA* 45:524$_{10}$f.; *LW* 24:); *Predigt in Halle gehalten,* January 6, 1546 (*WA* 51:113$_{5f}$8); *Against Hanswurst,* 1541 (*WA* 51:487$_{24–28}$; *LW* 41:199); *Against the Roman Papacy, an Institution of the Devil,* 1545 (*WA* 54:266$_{18–22}$; *LW* 41:336); Thomas Aquinas, *Summa theologiae,* II, 2, Question 189, Article 3.

Wittenberg Concord. A compromise statement on Protestant understandings of the sacraments. Representatives of both the southern and the northern German Protestants signed WC at Wittenberg in May of 1536.

WC played an important role in the historical context surrounding the formulation of SA.

Word of God. Galatians 1:8. FCEp, Introduction, 1. *Ein Sermon gepredigt zu Leipzig auf dem Schloss am Tage Petri und Pauli,* 1519 (*WA* 2:427$_{8ff.}$); *Assertio omnium articulorum M. Lutheri per bullam Leonis X,* 1520 (*WA* 7:131–33); and *Defense and Explanation of All Articles,* 1521 (*WA* 7:423–27; *LW* 32:76–79); Sermons on the Gospel of John, Chapters 1–4, 1537 (*WA* 46:781; *LW* 22:266).